Jada

Kindred Spirit
Unconditional Love Series
Vol. II

By
Yvonne L. James

Copyright © 2016 by Yvonne L. James

Jada
Kindred Spirit
Unconditional Love Series
Vol. II
by Yvonne L. James

Printed in the United States of America.

ISBN 9781498465359

All rights reserved solely by the author. The author guarantees all contents are original and do not infringe upon the legal rights of any other person or work. No part of this book may be reproduced in any form without the permission of the author. The views expressed in this book are not necessarily those of the publisher.

Scripture quotations taken from the King James Version (KJV) – *public domain*

www.xulonpress.com

Acknowledgements

I wish to personally thank the following people
for their contribution to my inspiration and knowledge
and other help in creating this book.

My Brother, Pastor John L. Lewis III,
My Dear Friend, Elder Lynn Goebel and
My Daughter, Taniea Shevonne Reynolds

God Bless You! Love you guys, Unconditionally!

TABLE OF CONTENTS

Acknowledgements v
Foreword xi
Dedication xiii

Chapter I	Keeping The Faith	17
Chapter II	The Big Apple	26
Chapter III	As The World Turns	40
Chapter IV	Life Changes	45
Chapter V	The Past Returns	49
Chapter VI	Lost And Found	55
Chapter VII	The Secret	65
Chapter VIII	One Plus One Equals One	72
Chapter IX	Shocking Discovery	81
Chapter X	The Reveal	87
Chapter XI	A New Life	95
Chapter XII	Favor Is Forever	102
Chapter XIII	Love Prevails	109

Chapter XIV	Love Everlasting	117
Chapter XV	God's Promises	124
Chapter XVI	Great Job!	134
Chapter XVII	Second Chances	139
Chapter XVIII	Missing	147
Chapter IXX	The Last Piece Of The Puzzle	154
What Is Sarcoidosis?		159

UNCONDITIONAL LOVE SERIES

1. Love Unconditionally
2. JADA

FOREWORD

By

Pastor Michael Tyree

Faith Christian Outreach Center

Winston Salem, North Carolina

*I*f you like PASSION, ROMANCE AND SUSPENSE! Then you will love *"JADA!"* As you read this book, together you and Jada will take an exciting journey through her life's many challenges. You'll also see her display a tremendous hope and loving faith to conquer and overcome these challenges.

When I think about "Unconditional Love", I think about a display of genuine love that comes from the heart; with "no strings attached." The only true example of this kind of Unconditional Love we have, is that "Agape Love" shown by our heavenly Father. In spite of our many faults, failures and disobedient acts against Him; He found a way to forgive us and love us "anyway!" You'll find that type of love, faith, and forgiveness displayed throughout Jada's story.

So, whether you're a shopping clerk at Wal-Mart, a prestigious attorney at a well to do law firm, or just a person who loves to read, you'll be glued to the pages of "Jada" as her story unfolds right before your very eyes. So be prepared to cry a little...to smile a little, and to love a lot, as you read "Jada" — the second book in the "Unconditional Love Series" by Yvonne L. James.

DEDICATION

I would like to dedicate this book to my husband Richard Leon "Casey" James (Deceased 12.19.2015), my Father, John L. Lewis, Jr (Deceased) and my Mother Christine Lewis, who taught me the true meaning of loving unconditionally. Also, to my brother's Roderick Sr, Dallas (Deceased), and John L. III: My sister Lola: My children; Lawrence, Taniea, Casey, Sheree, Richard and Terry: My very special niece Tammi, My nieces Regina, Trisha, Nacobi, and Shannon: My grandchildren; Marquel, Giovonni, Adant`e, Kian, Samara, A`yauna, Jhamya, Jazmyn, Mark, Alveno, Joshua, Jarrett, Janelle, Quentin, Sydney, Niccoli, Bailey, and Nakesha: My nephnews; Roderick Jr, John IV, Jeremy, and Darius. Thank you all and I love you all....................

UNCONDITIONALLY!

*A special thank you to
Archer Photography
Kansas City, MO*

Yvonne Lyn Lewis James

CHAPTER 1

Matthew 25:21
"His lord said unto him,
Well done, thou good and faithful servant:
Thou hast been faithful over a few things, I will make thee
ruler over Many things, enter thou into the joy of thy lord"

KEEPING THE FAITH

No one knows what God has planned for their lives, and Jada McCormick was no exception. She knew she had to keep praying to fulfill God's plan in her life and she knew she had to depend on God in every aspect of her life. As strong as her faith was, she had no doubt that God would always work on her behalf. She had seen God do so many things in her life and she knew He wouldn't let her down now.

As the sun tops the mountain tops that she can see in a distance over the tall buildings, on another beautiful day, Jada climbs out of bed and starts getting ready for her day. As she glances out of the window, a smile comes upon her face as she hears the birds sing and sees the sun bounce off the tops of the trees afar off. She is thinking, "What a beautiful day." As she watches the sun rise over the top of the highest building in the city which is about 10 miles from the mountains where the beautiful sun tops the trees, she stretches and thanks God for letting her see another day. She slowly slids herself to the edge of the bed, places her feet into her slippers, and stands to her feet with a sigh. Jada makes her way to the shower; floating past the dresser to turn on the radio.

After her shower, she makes her way downstairs to get coffee going, then back upstairs to get dressed and put on her makeup. Jada then heads back to the kitchen for coffee, until she looks at the clock and notices the time is getting late. She throws the morning paper under her arm, grabs her briefcase, purse, and coffee, and is out the door. As she backs out of the garage, she says good morning to her neighbor, Mr. Black, who is jogging by, just like he does every morning.

When she gets to the interstate, she notices that the traffic is really congested today. As she gets closer to work, she realizes that she is going to be running a little late, so Jada calls her boss to let him know she is on her way. As she approaches the cause of the congestion, she notices a little girl lying on the ground. The child has been hit by a truck, and emergency vehicles have the road blocked. How did this baby, who looks no more than six years old, now helpless and limp, get into the street alone, Jada wonders, where are the parents of this precious baby?

Jada passes the accident, pauses a moment to pray for the little girl, asking God that she be all right and for a full, back-to-normal recovery for her, before going on to work.

Jada is a lawyer with Lewis & Associates, a very prestigious law firm in Atlanta, Georgia. She has been with the firm for about three years and is already in line for a promotion. Everything is finally falling into place for her, and she couldn't be any happier than she is at this moment, with the way things are going in her life. At one point, it seems as if her whole life is going wrong, but she keeps depending on God until a brighter day comes along.

Jada had an uncle who lived in Buckhead, Georgia that passed away, which is how she ended up in Buckhead. She went to Buckhead when her Uncle Blake passed away to take care of his affairs. It is really nice in Buckhead, and she fell in love with the place. She loves it so much she has decided not to sell her uncle's house. She will make Buckhead her home.

"Jada"

Her life is in shambles at the time of her move to Buckhead. It just might be a blessing in disguise. Her mother passed away six months prior to her move. Three months after her mother passed, her uncle Blake passed away. She is at such a loss and doesn't know what to do. She was very close to her uncle Blake. She is going to truly miss him. She feels at this time in her life that a piece of her is gone. She feels so alone now. Her Mom and her uncle are gone. But, there is something else that is botherering her too. It is the fact that she found out three months after her mother's death that her position in the company is being faded out. The company is having a lot of downsizing. Because she is the newest kid on the block, her position is in jeopardy. She has only been with the company for nine months, so of course she will be the first to go.

Also, three months prior to her move to Buckhead, she and her husband Jerald were divorced... after seven years of marriage.

After her divorce was final, she started to reminisce about her past. She doesn't live in the past, because she wants to go on with her life living for the future, but, there is something that really plagues her and keeps dragging her back. It is the fact that her parents divorced when she was about three years old, and she didn't have a chance to really get to know her father. His name is Dana, and he now lives in New York. That's all she knows.

She misses that father daughter time that she so deeply wishes she'd had. She prays every day that one day she'll get to meet him and really get to know him. Then, one day, maybe they can form a relationship that is so long overdue.

Jada used to ask her mother about her father, but she would always change the subject and not want to talk about him. I guess it hurt too much for her to talk about him, or for some other unknown reason she doesn't know about. Her mother never wanted her to mention his name.

Jada always wanted to know what happened to cause her parents to divorce. Do you just stop loving someone that you have been with for so long? Hopefully, one day she'll know what went wrong. Her father has the answers, this is why she so desperately wants to find him so she can hear what he has to say.

She can't understand why her father has never tried to get in touch with his only child. She has so many questions. Did he remarry? Does she have other brothers and sisters? Was she the cause of the divorce? Did he not want her or just didn't love her? Did he not like her because she wasn't a boy? These are questions she has that only her dad can answer.

As Jada enters the law firm she goes straight to her office. When she gets to her desk, she finds a note from her boss;

Jada,

Please come to my office when you arrive.

Mr. Dent.

Now Jada is curious. What is this all about? Is this more bad news? She can't take any more bad news, not now. Oh boy! Now what?! She feels that a prayer is in order for this one. She sits down at her desk, puts her head in her hands and starts to pray.

After she prays, she slowly walks to Mr. Dent's office. This is the longest walk she has ever taken down this narrow hallway. As she walks down the hallway, she can feel her heart beating so hard and even hear it pounding very loud. It is beating so fast that she thinks it's going to pop right out of her chest.

She knocks on the big cherry wood door with three quick raps. Her knees knock louder than she knocks does on that door. On the other side of the door a deep, husky, but gentle voice says;

"Come in."

As she enters the office and closes the door behind her, she is still walking like she is in a trance.

"Mr. Dent, you want to see me?"

Mr. Dent looks up and smiles at her.

"Yes I do. Please, have a seat Jada."

As she sits down, very slowly in the chair, she can't imagine what he wants with her. She is on pins and needles. Her heart is beating 200 beats a minute while she holds her breath, waiting for him to say something.

"Jada,....he says in a deep voice....I've been watching you, and you are doing a fabulous job."

Jada takes a deep breath of relief but she is still puzzled. "Thank you Mr. Dent."

"I think it's time for you to move up to something more challenging." He looks at her up over his glasses and seems to look right through her. "I have a case I would like you to take on." He leans back in his chair, takes his glasses off and starts chewing on the tip of them.

"This is a murder case and it involves a 12 year old boy. His name is Donnavon Black. It' a big one and I want you to have it. This can be a big help with your promotion if you win this one. Do you think you can handle it?"

"Yes I can Mr. Dent. I would love to give it my best shot. I guarantee you a win."

Mr. Dent looks at her, smils, and leans back in his chair. He crosses his arms and tilts his head to one side. "I know you will. I know you can do it."

"OOOOOH GEEE THANKS! Thanks a lot Mr. Dent!! That doesn't put any pressure on me at all!"

They both laugh as she gets up and leaves his office

Five o'clock…the end of the day… has finally come. Jada can't wait to get home, put her feet up, relax, and prepare for the weekend so she can get started researching and working on the case. She has a lot on her plate now.

Jada makes her way through the busy traffic finally getting home. Now that she's finally home she can rest for a few minutes. She has had cases like robbery, assault, forgery, embezzlement, now she is adding a murder case. This case will be a breakthrough for her.

Donavon is in jail for murder and attempted murder. The other victim is in ICU still unconscious, in critical condition. She doesn't have his name yet, but she'll get it when she's finally able to talk to him, if he survives. He has been in a coma since the attack, so information is impossible to get at this time. She can only pray that he comes out of the coma to shed some light on the case. If he dies, Donnavon will be charged with two counts of murder. Something she doesn't want to see.

After viewing the case, she realizes this case takes her to leads in Missouri, New York, and Chicago. As she researches the case further, she finds out it seems that there were three other men involved, but Donnavon is the youngest. He was supposed to be the trigger man in this inc

As she gathers information on the case, she comes across some interesting evidence that makes her ask the question...."God, where were you in this fiasco? I am not questioning your will God; I am just saying; this is a child, a baby. I know there is something here I'm not seeing. God, please reveal it to me. There has to be something I'm missing, you better believe I'm going to find it with your help."

Jada has books and papers all over the bed and kitchen table, trying to find something that will give her some leads. She thinks hard and long then decides she is going to make a call and take a trip to New York as soon as possible to talk to one of the other men involved in this gruesome incident.

CHAPTER II

Matthew 5:21
"Ye have heard that it was said by them of old time
Thou shalt not kill; And whosoever shall kill shall be
in danger of the judgment:"

The Big Apple

*J*ada decides to take the last flight to New York so she can get an early start the following morning. She goes to her room and packes her bags and purchases her ticket.

She arrives at the airport... running a little late as usual... she parkes in short term parking so she won't have to worry about getting a taxi.. She gatheres all of her things then gets her suitcase from the trunk. She runs through the airport to catch her flight. She is never on time for flights. As she finally reaches the gate and boards her flight, she has a thousand things going through her head. She really wants to get this young man off, she knows she has her work cut out for her.

The Big Apple

She is determined to prove he is innocent. She feels deep in her heart that he is not guilty.

There is a bad thunderstorm when she lands at the airport in New York. She makes her way through the airport running, dragging her luggage behind her, talking on her cell phone and looking for the exit. As she approaches the doorway she is looking behind her when she collides with a man that is also rushing through the door. When they collide, they drop everything in the floor. As they bend down to retrieve their belongings they look in each others eyes.

"I am so sorry, said Jada."

"Oh! No! It's my fault! I shouldn't have been running like that. My name is Troy, Troy Mason. Are you okay?"

"Yes, I am fine, thank you for asking."

"Here is my card. Call me if you are hurt. I'll be back in town tomorrow night, staying at the Lenox Hotel, room 337. As a matter of fact, call me regardless. Please."

"Okay, I'll do that Troy". She looks at the card he gave her. "I see you are an attorney Troy."

"Yes I am. Do you need my help"?

They both laugh and start on their way.

"No, not yet. But I might, so don't go far".

"I won't."

Both of them laugh and kept going.

"By the way, my name is Jada… Jada Lawson."

They laugh again as they get farther apart.

"Thank you so much sir."

"You are most welcome Madam."

As they continue on their way, Troy is looking back, walking fast…almost a trot… looking at Jada, almost collides with a man in the terminal.

"Excuse me sir, this is not my day."

"No problem, no harm done".

Jada grabs a taxi and heads to the hotel to get ready for the next morning. She checks into the hotel, unpacks, and orders room service. While she is eating she makes a few phone calls to make some appointments. That night, Jada rests for the day she has coming up. The next morning she has an appointment with Joshua Mackey, one of the other men involved in the case. She gets a wakeup call at 6:00 am, orders breakfast, gets into the shower, and pust her robe on to wait on room service. When her breakfast arrives she has an hour and a half to eat and get ready for her appointment. She quickly eats her breakfast, gets dressed, and rushes downstairs to get a taxi to the jail to meet with Joshua. When she

The Big Apple

arrives at the jail she has to go through checkpoints, which is required to visit inmates.

She finally gets in to talk to Joshua and finds out a lot of things she doesn't know. The first thing she finds out is ... Joshua is sitting in the car and he doesn't know what is about to take place inside the house. He thinks Darrin is going to visit his uncle for a minute. He has no idea Darrin is going to rob and kill anyone. He also tells her Donnavon goes in to use the restroom and he doesn't know what is going to take place either. Joshua says he hears the shots and runs inside to see what is going on. When he gets inside and sees two bodies lying on the floor. He is in a state of shock. Donnavon is standing there by the television in shock and Darrin is yelling at him to get the two men's money so they can get out of there. Donnavon finally comes to his senses and yells back at Darrin.

"WHAT HAVE YOU DONE DARRIN!!!!?? HAVE YOU LOST YOUR MIND!!!!?? THIS IS YOUR UNCLE'S HOUSE, YOUR UNCLE!!! AND YOU SHOOT YOUR UNCLE!!!?? ARE YOU CRAZY!!??"

"I WILL SHOW YOU HOW CRAZY I AM IF YOU DON'T HURRY UP SO WE CAN GET OUT OF HERE?!! AND THIS IS NOT MY UNCLE'S HOUSE!!!"

"Jada"

"That is what I am seeing when I go into the house. Donnavon is innocent. He didn't pull the trigger, Darrin did."

"Okay, thank you Joshua this is going to be a big help. I have one question for you though. Did you know these people that lived in the house?"

"No! I didn't! And neither did Donnavon. I don't know if Darrin did."

"Thank you so much Joshua. We'll talk again soon."

No one knows where Darrin is….they only know he is in New York. Jada has to find him and find him quick. She leaves the prison and goes to the police station to see what she can find out. Lieutenant Kramer is in charge of the investigation on this case. She gpes to his office to talk to him and finds out they have an all points bulletin out for Darrin. They promise to let her know when they find out something. Before she leaves the office, they get a call about a break-in and shooting downtown, and Lt. Kramer has to leave and go to the scene of the shooting. On her way to the hotel she gets a phone call to come back to the police station. When she arrives, Lt. Kramer is waiting for her. He lookes at her with a strange look in his eyes.

"The shooting I told you about, I think we got your man. It is Darrin."

Jada asked to talk to him. When she goes in to talk to Darrin he is cooperative and tells her the whole story about the murder. The boys were telling the truth, they are innocent. Now, she only has to get the jury to believe it. They still have another victim to think about, the man in the coma. Jada got permission to go see him in ICU.

When she gets to the hospital, she goes right to the unit to see this man. She walks in and stands over the bed and looks down at him lying lifeless there in front of her. She stares at him and can't put her finger on it, but, there is something about this man that pulls on her. Is he trying to tell her who did this to him? She sure wants him to wake up. He is really the only credible witness they have. They still don't have a name because there is no identification on him when he is found and he isn't the owner of the house. This they do know. When she leaves the hospital she leaves her contact information with administration and the nursing supervisor in case he comes out of the coma.

She goes back home to start working on a defense for Donnavon and Joshua. Yes, she takes on Joshua's case too. She tells Mr. Dent what she finds out while in New York and he is very pleased. Now all she has to do is get these boys out

"Jada"

of jail. She has to hurry and get her defense together because the trial starts in two days.

It's trial day for Jada and the boys are very scared. They were in the wrong place at the wrong time with the wrong people. Her first murder trial and it can turn out to be a double homicide.

Lt. Kramer brings Darrin to Georgia to testify. The jury comes to a quick decision of not guilty. Darrin, on the other hand, is in big trouble. She wanted to take on his case too but he has a lawyer already. His trial will start in a couple of weeks.

Jada has a busy day in court and goes home to relax. She sits down and starts cleaning out her purse and runs across Troy's business card. She decides to give him a call.

"Troy, this is Jada. Remember, we ran into each other at the airport? Literally....." and they both laugh.

"Yes, I remember you. How have you been doing?"

"I am doing great...busy though."

"Yeah, I know what you mean. What do I owe the pleasure of this call?"

"I was looking through some things and found your card and decided to give you a call. Is that okay?"

"Sure it is. Would you like to go have coffee with me and relax, or maybe dinner?"

"Troy, are you here in Georgia?"

"Yes I am, I live in Georgia."

"Troy, how did you know I live in Georgia?"

"I didn't know, I asked around. You can find anything if you ask questions. You know that." They both laugh.

"As a matter of fact, hold on just a minute…..got it! My computer says that you live about six blocks from me."

"What a coincidence, she says. I can't go though. I have an important case I'm working on."

"You still need to relax Jada. Come on, it's only coffee."

"Okay, you're right. I will meet you at the Coffee Shop on 3rd. Is that okay?"

"Yes ma'am. I'll see you there in about 30 minutes."

"Okay, see you then".

Jada arrives at the Coffee Shop about ten minutes before Troy arrives. She orders water for both of them and has the waitress wait for about five minutes before bringing coffee. When Troy arrives, he has one purple rose. When he hands it to her, she smiles and thanks him.

"This is a beautiful rose. Where did you get such a beautiful thing?"

"I found it outside at a little shop about a block away. It was sitting there calling your name. Please don't think I'm flirting with you because I'm not. I just wanted to break the ice and maybe relax you. Please don't take it wrong."

"I don't. Thank you so much. This is a real sweet gesture."

They have coffee and talk for almost three hours. They find out a lot about each other too. He has to go to Detroit on Tuesday to talk to a client. She didn't know that he is Darrin's lawyer. New York has Darrin sent back to Detroit for a crime there he has committed.

After he gets back from Detroit, he calls Jada and they get together for dinner and a movie. They really enjoy each others company and always have a lot to talk about. This is their chance to get away from work and just relax. They have gotten very close in the last few months. Will this be the love that Jada is looking for or will this be just another fling that only lasts for a little while?

She and Troy are at dinner when her phone rings. It is Nurse Rachel from New York General Hospital. She calls to inform Jada that Mr. John Doe has finally come out of the coma and is trying to talk a little. Jada hangs up the phone and tells Troy what the call is about. She lets him know she is going to have to fly to New York.

The Big Apple

"Jada, would you like me to accompany you to New York?"

"No Troy. Thank you so much, but I will be okay alone."

When she arrives at the hospital, Nurse Rachel is in his room cleaning him up.

"Has he said anything?"

"He only told us his name so far."

"What is his name?"

"We only have DJ."

"Okay, thanks a lot."

Jada walks over to the bed and calls him a couple of times. "DJ? DJ?"

He turns his head, opens his eyes, and looks up at her.

"Hi DJ, my name is Jada. I want to help you. I'm an attorney and I want to find out who hurt you. Do you understand what I'm saying?"

He slowly nodded his head yes.

"DJ, can you tell me your last name?"

He nods yes. He slowly drags out "Jaaa.....Jaaa."

Jada interrupts him. "Don't strain yourself DJ. I'll get it later. It isn't important right now."

She holds his hand as he looks up at her, then he slowly closes his eyes and falls asleep. She feels so connected to him. Is it because the suspect is so young? What is the connection she has for this stranger? She can't put her finger on it but she will figure it out.

As she leaves the room she ask the nurse to keep her informed about his condition.

"If he says anything else, please call me. It doesn't matter what time of day or night, call me."

She promises to let her know if there is any change in his condition. Jada heads back to the hotel to rest so she can get a fresh start the next morning.

When Jada leaves DJ's room she tells him she will be back later that day. She has to check some things out concerning the case. As she leaves, she is walking in a daze. She has so many unanswered questions. The main question is, what is the connection between her and this man she just met? He is pulling on her and she needs him to pull through.

Jada makes several trips to New York to talk to DJ, Donnavon, and Joshua. She is also going to the house where the crime takes place to see if she can find out anything, or if something's been missed. On her last visit to New York, DJ is going to be released from the hospital. His memory still hasn't completely returned but it will eventually. She takes him home, gets him settled in, and calls a therapist for him so he can get his therapy started. He is doing quite well...considering what he has been through.

Jada finally makes it back to Georgia. She starts preparing for the trial that s to take place in a couple of weeks. DJ is going to appear at the trial to face the young men that supposedly attacked him. Jada has worked so hard on their defense. She is certain that she will be able to get the boys off because they are innocent, but, they were there when the crime takes place, and they didn't tell the police what happened. This will be held against them.

It is trial day and DJ has arrived at the court house. Jada meets him and escortes him to chambers where he can relax. He is still recovering but doing very well. The trial finally gets underway, they call a couple of witnesses to the stand before they call DJ. When they put DJ on the stand, he sits down, looks out over the crowd, his eyes stop at the boys that have been accused of killing his friend, and leaving him to die. He can't believe that two young boys can be so involved in such a serious crime. His eyes stay on Donnavon for some reason, but he just can't figure out why he looks so familiar.

The Prosecutor and Jada question DJ for about 30 minutes. They find out a lot of information they don't know. He did tell them that the boys seated in front of him was not who pulled the trigger. He also describes Darrin to a tee. DJ's story about the incident matches what Darrin has told Jada previously. Now what are the jury and the judge going to do? We just have to wait and see.

Jada calls Troy to see if he can have coffee with her while she is waiting for the verdict. He agrees to meet her at a little coffee shop in ten minutes.

"Hey Jada. How's it going? How did the verdict come out?"

"I am waiting on it now. I don't think it is going to take long. At least I pray it doesn't."

"They are going to be found innocent. You watch and see. There is no way they will be found guilty of murder, considering the

circumstances. It'll be okay, you'll see."

"I hope you're right Troy. I really hope you're right."

While they are talking and drinking their coffee, Jada's phone rings. It's the court house. They tell her the jury is back and she needs to come back immediately. Both of them get up and go to the courthouse to see how things turn out.

The way it turns out is really good for the boys. They could be doing some serious jail time. Donnavon gets six months in Juvenile Detention, with time served. Because Joshua helped with the case, he gets six months in jail, with time served. He only has to serve three months of his time. So everything is turning out well for the boys. Hopefully, the boys have learned a lesson and will pick their friends more carefully.

God really worked on their behalf this time. Now Jada can go tell Mr. Dent how things turned our and see where it takes her. She can't wait to see the look on his face when she tells him she won the case and how well it went. He will be well pleased with her.

CHAPTER III

Romans 8:28
"And we know that all things work together for good to them that Love God, to them who are the called according to his Purpose"

AS THE WORLD TURNS

Jada has the weekend to rest up after the court hearing with the boys before going back to work. She can't wait to get back to work so she can talk to Mr. Dent about the case. This is one of the proudest moments in her career. As she sits on her sofa watching a movie, she stares at the phone for ten minutes then said:

"I can't hold it any longer, I have to call him."

She runs across the room and dials his number. As she waits for the rings to stop, the excitement mounts. At the other end she finally hears:

"Hello."

As The World Turns

"Hello Mr. Dent this is Jada."

"Hi Jada, how can I help you and how did it go in New York?"

"Mr Dent, I have to tell you this wasn't an easy case."

"Oh no! You lost the case, didn't you?"

"Mr. Dent"...... she hesitates......

"Don't worry Jada, you will have another chance."

"But Mr. Dent, you don't understand, I won the case!!"

"Jada!!! That's great!!! I am so proud of you. Can you meet me for lunch tomorrow to celebrate?"

"Sure! Where shall I meet you?"

"How about meeting at the Bantoon Restaurant at noon?"

"That's great! I will see you then! Have a good night."

"Thank you and you too."

"Oh.....congratulations again."

"Thank you, good night."

"Good night Jada."

Jada is feeling fabulous now. A big weight has been lifted off of her shoulders because she couldn't wait all weekend to tell Mr. Dent about the case.

While Jada and Mr. Dent were having lunch it was the proudest moment she has ever had. Mr. Dent is so proud of her. They talk and laugh the whole time they are having lunch. They just have a marvelous time together. While they are eating, a good friend walks into the restaurant. It is Troy Mason. Jada hasn't seen him in a while because he has been out of town at a trial. Although they do talk on the phone, that isn't the same as being there.

"Troy! Troy!" she yells across the room. No time for etiquette now. At least not for Jada.

"Hi Jada! I had no idea I would see you here. How have you been?"

"I have been great. Troy this is my boss, Mr. Dent. Mr. Dent this is Troy Mason, a good and dear friend of mine."

"Hello Mr. Dent. Nice to meet you," says Troy.

"Same here young man. Won't you join us?"

"Sure. Thank you. I was just going to grab a bite to eat and then go in for the night."

"Great! Have a seat, says Jada."

"Troy I am just updating Mr. Dent on the case I just finished."

"Oh yes! Mr. Dent you must be very proud of her."

"Yes I am. Very proud!"

The evening goes very well for the three of them and they decide to call it a night. Mr. Dent goes home and Troy and

Jada decide to go dancing at "The Palace" to celebrate her winning the biggest case she has ever had.

They dance until late in the morning and Jada decides it is time to turn in for the night. Troy walks her to her car and watches her drive off until her tail lights are out of sight.

Troy thinks about Jada all night and she is the first thing on his mind when he gets up that morning. He is wondering... what is this? Why am I feeling this way about this woman? What is it about her that I can't get her off of my mind? I have been in love before...I think.....but this is different. What is this I am feeling? It isn't a bad feeling but he wonders if Jada is feeling the same way he is. He is going to find out because he is going to ask her when they go to dinner.

Troy gets up, gets dressed and heads out for his morning run. After his run he showers, gets dressed then decides to call Jada. Jada doesn't answer her phone. So he assumes she must be on her way to work.

When Jada arrives at work, the co-workers greet her with confetti, balloons, and cake to celebrate her victory. Mr. Dent has told them about Jada winning the biggest case the firm has had in a long time. Jada is so happy she hugs on everybody, laughs, even cries as she tries to put her things down on her desk. They bombard her with love, congratulations, cards, you can't imagine the joy in that office.

After things settled down she notices that the message light on her phone is blinking. It's a message from Troy. She listens to it and calls him back before she gets settled down to work.

"Hi Troy! I am sorry I missed your call. What's up?"

"Hi Jada! I just want to know if I can take you to lunch….. well make that dinner too. I want to talk to you about something."

"Oh my God! Troy, is something wrong?"

"No… No… No… No! Calm down! Breathe Jada! Everything is fine! I just want to discuss Us with you."

"US?" asks Jada.

"Yes, us."

"Okay Troy, we can do lunch and dinner too. Dinner depends on what the "Us" is about. What time shall we meet and where?"

"I will pick you up at noon. Is that okay?"

"Yes it is. I will be waiting."

"Okay, great. I will see you later."

"Okay, later."

CHAPTER IV

1 John 1:9
*"If we confess our sins, he is faithful
and just to forgive us our sins,
And to cleanse us from all unrighteousness."*

Life Changes

  *J*ada has no idea what Troy wants to talk about with her. She is really curious, even somewhat afraid of what is on his mind. As she prepares herself for lunch with Troy, she is becoming very anxious.

  Troy arrives to pick her up at noon as planned. She is in Mr. Dent's office when he arrives so he takes a seat until she comes out. He waits about five minutes before she comes out of the office and they can leave for lunch.

  "Oh! Hi Troy. I am so sorry for my tardiness. There was something Mr. Dent wanted to discuss with me."

"That's okay Jada. We all have a job to do. Are you ready to go now?"

"Yes, I am," she replies.

"Shall we," utters Troy.

"Let's," she lovingly says.

Troy opens the car door and Jada slids into the seat. As they drive to the restaurant, Jada keeps looking at Troy.

"What's wrong Jada?"

"I'm curious about what you want to talk to me about."

Troy stops the car in front of the restaurant, gets out of the car, opened the door for her to get out, reaches for her hand to help her out of the car, then leades her into the restaurant.

The waiter seats them then brings them something to drink.

"Well Troy, what is it that you want to talk to me about?"

"Jada, we have been seeing each other for a while now and I am wondering if you feel the same way I do about us?"

"And what way is that, Troy?"

"Well, Jada…I have grown very fond of you. I like you a lot, I care a great deal about you Jada. You are always in my thoughts. You are the first thing I think about when I get up in the morning and the last thing I think about when I go to bed at night. I breathe you Jada."

Life Changes

"Troy, I thinking it is only me feeling this way. I was afraid to say anything to you because I didn't know if you were feeling the same way about me. I'm thinking I'm in this alone."

"Oooooh, Jada, you are not alone....I do feel the same way you do. It's time for me to get you back to work. Can we finish this conversation after work?"

"Yes we can, Troy."

"Can I stop by your house this evening around 8:00? I have to work late and won't get off until them."

"Sure. I'll be waiting."

Troy goes by Jada's after work to finish his talk with her. Jada has some hors d'oeuvres with coffee prepared for them. Troy shows up with a boutique of purple and white roses and a bottle of champagne, non-alcoholic of course. Jada greets him at the door with a hug, kiss on the cheek, then looks into his eyes. He kisses her on the forhead then comes into the house after handing her the flowers.

"Jada, should I put this champagne on ice for you?"

"Yes. Please do that for me while I put these beautiful roses in a vase. Thank you so much for these. They are beautiful!"

"You are so welcome. Beauty desearves beauty."

"That is so sweet Troy. Thank You."

"Jada, I really want to be with you and only you. I havn't felt this way about anyone for a long time. As I matter of fact, I have never felt this way about anyone, and it is a bit frightening for me."

"I know what you mean Troy. It's been a long time for me too. Not only a long time, but my last relationship was a bad one, and because of that, I kind of shyed away from serious relationships. But, I trust you with my heart Troy, so where will we go from here?"

"We can become an item if you will have me, then we will see where it goes from here."

"Sounds good to me." says Jada.

He took her in his arms, kissed her, then they start to watch a movie on television.

Months are going by. Jada and Troy are still together, still doing well, their jobs are great, winning case after case, doing a lot of traveling, even working some cases together. They can't ask for anything better. A dream come true!

CHAPTER V

Joel 2:25
"And I will restore to you the years that the locust hath eaten, the Cankerworm, and the caterpiller, and the palmerworm, my great Army which I sent among you."

The Past Returns

One day while Jada is coming out of the court house she runs into and old client. It is DJ. She never really knew his real name because he only knew DJ at the time of the trial. He hadn't gotten his memory back before the trial was over and Jada had finished working on his case. She lost contact with him after that until today. She calls out to him.

"DJ? Is that you?"

"Hey! Jada! How are you?" He hugs her and they continue to talk.

"I am great! How are you doing?" She replies anxiously.

"Good! Is everything going ok for you?" asks DJ.

"Yes it is. By the way, I don't knnow what your real name is I only know DJ."

"Oh, ok. My name is Dana….Dana Jordan."

Jada looks so shocked and her face freezes..

"Jada, are you alright?! Is something wrong?!"

"No. No. I, I, I, I'mmmm fine. Caaaaaan I get your number so I can call you some time?"

"Sure. It's 712.345.5645. You can call me any time. Are you sure you're okay?"

"Yes. I'm sure I'm, okay DJ, I will call you soon. It is good seeing you again."

"You too Jada. Have a good day."

To her surprise, she thinks she has found her Father. She is going to check things out to make sure, but she knows this man they call Dana Jordan, or DJ, is her father. She can't believe that a tragedy like this one is going to turn into something good. Or is it a good thing? She is in a state of shock but she is also happy about it. She can't wait to talk to Troy about him to see what he has to say.

When Jada gets home she makes a call to Troy to ask him over, because she has something important to talk to him about. She is sure she has found her father but she doesn't know what to do about it right now.

The Past Returns

When Troy arrives, she is so anxious he has to calm her down before they can talk.

"What is wrong sweetheart? Talk to me."

"Troy, the strangest thing happrned to me today."

"What?"

"I am coming out of the courthourse and run into DJ. Do you remember him?"

"Yes I do. Go on."

"He tells me his name was Dana Jordan."

"Okay Jada, what does all of this mean?"

"Troy, my fathers name is Dana Jordan."

"Ooooh, I seeee. What are you getting at Jada?"

"I don't know. That's why I called you. Maybe you can help me find out if he is really my father before I make a fool of myself. I have been searching for so long. I want to have the right man. After all of these years is it possible that I have found my father? Troy, if I have, how do I tell him he's my dad? What will he say or how will he react? I'm afraid to confront him with it."

"Jada you have been waiting to long, you've looked to hard not to follow through with your hunch. You have to do this. Call him and set up a meeting with him. I'll go with you if you like."

"Jada"

"Oh yes Troy, please go with me! I would love that."

Jada calls DJ to set up a meeting for the next day at noon. She is so scared of what the outcome will be she can't sleep. She wants him to be her father but then again she doesn't. She is so confused and you can expect her to be.

Morning finally arrives and Jada starts her day as usual, trying to be as normal and as calm as she can be. Troy calls her to make sure she is okay and says he will pick her up at 11:00 to take her to the restaurant for their meeting with DJ.

As they approach the restaurant the more nervous Jada becomes. Troy parkes the car and tried to get her calmed down a bit before going inside to meet with DJ. He doesn't want her to scare afraid of him before he even knows what was going on. He finally gets her calmed down enough to go inside.

As the waiter takes them to their table, she is trembling so that Troy puts his arm around her to help calm hert. When they approach the table, Troy pulls out her chair while she sits down. She has a big smile on her face so big that it doesn't even look real.

"Hello DJ. How are you doing today?" ask Jada.

"I am great Jada. How are you Jada? Troy?"

"I am good." she says.

"I am well, thank you." replies Troy.

"Well Jada, what is this all about? Is something wrong?"

"Oh no DJ, nothing is wrong. I need to talk to you about something."

"Go ahead, I'm listening."

"DJ, I don't know any other way to say this but to come right out and say it. I don't want to sound too harsh but I know no other way to do it."

"What is it Jada"?

"DJ…..I think you are …….."

Jada pauses for a minute and DJ pushes her to finish the sentence.

"Go on Jada." pushes DJ.

"I think you are my father."

"What!?"

"Yes. My mothers name was Sarah. She told me my fathers name is Dana Jordan. She also said some other things about him that matches you exactly as she told me?"

"I'm not doubting you Jada. It's, it's just so shocking that we meet this way. I…. this is a lot to take in. I didn't know I would ever see you again. You were a baby when I left. My God!"

"You don't have to take my word for it. We can always get a DNA test done to make sure. I have looked through pictures, papers, everything I can find of my moms so I won't make a fool of myself when I bring this to you. I still don't know what to think or how I should feel."

Troy thinks it's about time he intervenes.

"Why don't the two of you go home, think about what has just been said then pick up on it again tomorrow."

"Yeah, that's a good idea." agreed Jada.

They all hugged then Jada and Troy left the restaurant. DJ.is still sitting there in a state of shock at the news he has just received.

CHAPTER VI

Psalms 3:4
"I cried unto the LORD with my voice,
And he heard me out of his holy hill." "Selah"

Lost And Found

*D*J can't believe after all these years that he has found the daughter that he walked away from 28 years ago. How is she going to feel about him? Better yet how is he going to feel about her? What and how is he going to tell his wife and kids about her? His family doesn't know about any other children he has. What is he going to do now?

DJ finally leaves the restaurant and goes for a long walk before going home to try to get his thoughts together. He feels a little bit better because he finally decides that all he can do is tell his family the truth.

He wants Jada in his life now. He has a chance to get to know her, he likes her a lot, now he wants to learn to love her, and love her as his daughter.

Jada on the other hand is a nervous wreck. She doesn't know how she feels about DJ. Is she still angry because he left her? Is she finally going to get her questions answered? Is she going to have the relationship she has always wanted with her father? Is he really her father? This is the question she really wants to get an answer to as quickly as possible, before moving on to anything else.

The next morning DJ calls Jada to find out if she is ready to go have a DNA test done. He wants to get it done because if he is her father, he wants to tell his family. He also wants to catch up with Jada the years that they have lost, if she will allow him to.

Jada is hesitant, but she agrees to go get it done. She wants to know and she doesn't want to know. She wants to know because she wants her father but she doesn't want to know because she is angry because he didn't love her enough to stay with her.

Jada is torn between loving him and hating him. She really is praying hard because she has never hated anyone before and she doesn't want to hate DJ either.

Troy picks Jada up the next morning to take her to the hospital to meet DJ.

When they arrive at the hospital, DJ is waiting for them.

"Good morning Jada. Are you ready for this?" ask DJ.

"Yes DJ, I'm ready. I am a little nervous, but let's get it over with."

"Okay Jada, lets go."

DJ reaches down, takes her by the hand and starts leading her down the hallway. Troy follows right beside them. He is such a great support to her at this time in her life. Jada looks at Troy as they walk down the hall. It seems like such a long walk.

Troy looks at her and assures her everything will be okay.

As they enter the room where the test is to be done, they are approached by the nurse.

"Dana Jordan and Jada Lawson?"

They both answer with a yes.

"Can you please follow me?"

They get up and follow the nurse to a room around the corner. As they get up, Jada turns to look at Troy. Troy tells her she can do this. DJ takes her by the hand, tells her she will be okay and he has her back.

"Jada"

The nurse performes the test then tells them the results will be ready in 24 hours. She will call them with the results or they can come in and pick them up. They decide to pick their results up. They think it will be quicker this way.

On the ride home Jada is very quiet. Troy ask her what she is thinking. She is wondering what it will be like if he is her father. Did she have other siblings? If so, will they accept her, get along with her, love her like she wants to love them. It will be a new life for all of them and it will be something they will have to get used to.

Troy tells Jada not to get too wound up. Take one step at a time. Let everything sink in and see what comes. Let God take control of the situation and make a way wantever it may be. He tells her she has to let God guide her steps and her words and she can't go wrong. He always has the right things to say at the right time.

Jada tosses and turns all night. She doesn't sleep at all and neither did DJ. As Jada looks over the tops of the trees and sees the sun top the mountain tops, she is still awake watching it rise. She gets up, showered and gets dressed. She goes downstairs and makes coffee, start breakfast, then calls Troy and DJ to see if they are up yet. She wants to invite them to over to have breakfast with her. Troy accepts but DJ makes up an excuse why he can't come. He can't explain to his wife why he is leaving that early in the morning.

As the morning grows late the more nervous Jada becomes. It is about 10:00 am. Troy tells Jada to call DJ to see if he is ready to go to the hospital to get their results. Jada does call him. He says he will meet them their.

As they arrive at the front door, DJ is already their waiting for them in the lobby. Dj grabs Jada's hand and says to her;

"Well Jada, this is it. We will soon know if I am your father or not. Are you ready?"

"Yes DJ. I am."

"Shall we?" he says.

He holds her hand tightly as they once again take that long walk down that long hallway. This time Troy goes with them all the way.

The nurse comes out and calls them into the room. She hands DJ an envelope and says:

"These are your results Mr. Jordan."

He hands the envelope to Jada. She hands it to Troy.

"Troy, can you please read them for us".

Troy opens the envelope and starts to read.

"DJ..... you are 99.99% ,.....Jada's father."

There is silence in the room for a few minutes. DJ is already holding Jada's hand, so he squeezes it tighter. Tears start to run down Jada's face. Troy has tears too. DJ has trouble fighting back the tears that are trying to cloud his eyes too.

What are the emotions in this room? Are they good ones or what are they? They get up and start to leave the room without saying a word. When they get to the lobby, Troy stops them.

"You can't leave this way. You have to say something to each other."

Jada looks at him and at DJ. She jerks her hand away from DJ and pushes him away from her and he almost hits the floor. Then she says:

"I DON'T HAVE TO SAY NOTHING! I TOLD YOU I WAS YOUR DAUGHTER! BUT NO! YOU HAVE TO HAVE A DNA TEST! YOU KNOW YOU HAVE A DAUGHTER NAMED JADA! I TOLD YOU AND YOU WANT TO ACT BRAND NEW!"

DJ speaks up but before he can get anything out, Jada slaps him so hard his teeth click and his whole body turns around.

"DON'T YOU SAY A WORD! I AM TALKING NOW! YOU LEFT ME AND ONLY THOUGHT ABOUT YOURSELF! YOU KNEW MY MOTHER WAS DOING

THINGS I SHOULDN'T BE AROUND! YOU WERE ONLY THINKING ABOUT YOURSELF! YOU CARED NOTHING FOR ME! NOW YOU WANT TO BE THE LOVING FATHER! YOU SHOULD HAVE TAKEN ME WITH YOU, BUT YOU LEFT ME BEHIND! A VERY SELFISH MOVE ON YOUR PART! YOU NEVER EVEN TRIED TO FIND ME! WHY!!!! I'M DONE WITH IT!!!

Jada turns to walk away and Troy grabs her hand and pulls her back.

Tears are still running down Jada's face.

DJ speaks up at this point.

"Jada, I can only say at this point that I am so sorry about everything. You don't know the whole story though. I did fight for you and your brother."

"WHAT! I HAVE A BROTHER! WHERE IS HE?!"

"When you are in a better place, I will tell you everything. I'm not disappointed that you are my daughter. We will get through this. We have been through enough for now Jada, I will call you later tonight. Is that okay?"

Jada just looks at DJ not saying a word. She turns and walks away, with Troy following behind her.

Later that evening DJ comes over to. Jada's to make sure she is alright. He is worried about her. Troy is with Jada because he doesn't want to leave her alone at this time in her life. They all go into the living room to sit down. Jada goes into the kitchen to get some lemonade.

DJ is a little hesitant but he starts the conversation with:

"There is something I need to tell you about me Jada. I am married. My wifes name is Candace. I also have two sons. Their names are Kevin and Traci. I haven't told them about you yet because I want to see what you want me to do, or how you want to handle this.

"I am not sure how I want to handle this right now".

"Okay, maybe you should sit them down and talk to them and not leave them in the dark the same way you did me. I can't believe I have two brothers. Oh! Excuse me! Three brothers! How old are they?"

"Kevin is 16 and Traci is 12. Jaden is the same age you are. Jada, Jaden is your twin brother."

"WOW! I have a twin brother! You have a lot of explaining to do! Where is he and why don't I know him? Why weren't we raised together?"

"Your mother wouldn't let me have you. She felt you should be with her because you were a girl and she thought Jaden would be better off with me. I know this is a lot to take in Jada and I am so sorry."

"SORRY!? THAT'S ALL YOU CAN SAY IS SORRY!? WHERE IS MY TWIN BROTHER DANA?! I'm a big sister to two! I hope they accept me. I will love to be in their life. But, what about us? You and me? Where does this leave us?"

"Where do you want it to leave us? What do you want of this relationship? Where do we go from here? It's up to you. I accept the fact that I am your father. I intend to do what a father is supposed to do."

"Now you want to be a father. Can you answer some questions for me?"

"If I can."

"Why did you leave me? Why didn't you get in touch with me in all those years? Do you not like girls? Is that why you took my brother and left me behind? Did you hate my mother so much that you hate me too?"

At this point the tears start to run down her face and she is sniffing like someone has just beaten her with their fist.

Troy sits down beside her, takes her in his arms and DJ drops his head in his hands and starts to answer her questions.

"Jada, Sweetheart, I loved your mother more that life itself. I never hated your mother or you. I loved you both so much that it hurt me to my heart to leave. I didn't get in touch because your mother wouldn't let me talk to you or see you. I already

"Jada"

told you about Jaden. In answer to your question…why did I leave you? I didn't leave you Jada, I left the life your mother made for us. I don't want to talk about your mother because she is gone now but you asked me, so here it is.

Your mother had started going around with other men and I couldn't take it anymore. I stayed as long as I could. I tried to take you with me but she wouldn't let me. Like I said, she felt you should stay with her and I should take Jaden. There was nothing else for me to do Jada. I'm sorry I left you but I had no other choice. I did try to find you after you turned 18 years old and again at 21, but I couldn't. I prayed that one day we would cross each others path and we did. God is good Jada and I pray you can forgive me for the years we've missed."

"I didn't know my mother was like that DJ. I'm sorry she treated you that way and caused the family to break up."

"Jada, your mother will always have a place in my heart. I will always love her and you don't owe me an apology, you did nothing wrong, that is how life is sometimes. Sometimes it works and sometimes it doesn't. You have to have God in it and let him do the choosing or you will make a mess of your life and others lives too. So make sure you hear from God when choosing a spouse, both of you."

CHAPTER VII

*"And he said unto him, Thy brother is come
and thy father hath killed the fatted calf
because he hath received him safe and sound."*

The Secret

When DJ returns home he is concerned about how his family will take the news about Jada. He ponders on how to tell them about his secret and decides to tell Candace first then together they will tell Kevin and Traci about Jada. That is, if Candace will agree to accept Jada into the family, and if she feels it would be okay to tell the boys at this time.

DJ calls Candace into the living room so he can talk to her. When Candace enters the room she sees the worry on his face and a very distraught look. She becomes very worried when she sees this. She can't imagine what is bothering him.

"Jada"

"Dana, what's wrong?" she ask with a concerned look.

"Candace, Honey, have a seat. I need to talk to you. I have something to tell you."

"Sweetheart, what is it? Is something wrong?"

"Noooo, Honey, everything is okay. I just have to tell you something."

"Baby, what is it?"

"Candace, before I met you......I was married before and had a daughter. It didn't work out with my wife, so we divorced when my daughter was about 2 years old. I never saw her again. That was about 24 years ago. When I was robbed a while back....you remember me telling you about that, right? Well anyway....she was the Lawyer for the young men who were involved."

"Oh yes, I do remember that. Go on."

"Well, I saw her a couple of weeks ago when she was coming out of the Court House. We stopped to talk and it turns out that we have some things in common. We know some of the same people. I was married to her mother. Candace..... she's my daughter. Her name is Jada Lawson."

"What!? Are you telling me you have a 26 year old daughter that I never knew anything about? Why are you telling me now?"

The Secret

"Candace, I just found out she's my daughter and this is the first time I have seen her since her mother and I split up. I am telling you now because I want her in our lives. I want to be a father to her like I have wanted to be but her mother wouldn't let me. I want you and the boys to accept her into the family and love her like I do. I didn't mean to keep anything from you, I just didn't know I would ever see her again. I thought she was lost to me forever. I am glad I found her Candace". He pauses for a minute waiting for a response from her.

"What are you thinking Babe? What do you have to say?"

"Dana, this is a lot to take in. Give me a minute. Please. I can't believe this. You kept this from me all this time. Why is this such a big secret?"

"I told you Candace. It isn't a secret, I just thought that part of my life was over and gone."

"Dana, a child is never over and gone! Have you lost you mind?! What are you thinking!?"

"I wasn't thinking Babe."

"I see. Well, I think this young lady deserves her family. It isn't her fault that her father is a jerk! I will tell the boys and prepare them so they won't be so shocked when they meet her. So, when do we meet her?"

"When do you want to meet her? I told her about you and she is excited about meeting all of you."

"Let me talk to the boys and you can invite her to dinner tomorrow. How's that?"

"That's fine. I'll ask Jada if she's available tomorrow, but I will wait until you talk to the boys to see how they feel. They might not be ready to meet her yet. I don't want to force Jada on them when they're not ready."

"Yes, you're right Dana. I'll talk to the boys today so we can get this out of the way and Jada can get on with her life."

"Thanks Babe, I really appreciate it." Dana calls Jada to set up dinner arrangements for her and Troy for the following day. But he did tell her he will make sure the plans are still on after they talk to the boys, but he wants to make sure she is free.

Candace sits the boys down to tell them what DJ has recently told her about Jada. Traci is all excited about having a sister but Kevin, he isn't too keen on the idea. He doesn't understand why he is just finding out about her and why she is such a secret. DJ explains everything he can about why he is just finding out about Jada, so he understands and accepts the situation better.

The Secret

DJ knows that in time he will grow to love Jada just like he loves his brother. All he has to do is get to know her. She will grow on him. No one can turn Jada away with those big pretty hazel eyes of hers, her enticing smile, and especially with dimples you can sink in. Time is going to change how he feels about her.

Dnner time rolls around the next evening. Dana is nervous about the meeting between his family and Jada. While he is watching TV the doorbell rings.

"Honey will you get the door please?" asked Candace.

"Sure Hon."

Dana gets up, goes to the door, of course it is Jada with Troy.

"Hi Jada, Troy, come in and have a seat."

"Hi DJ, thank you." they respond.

"You have a lovely home DJ."

"Thank you Jada."

While they are talking, Candace appears out of the foiyer and stands staring at Jada.

"Hello." says Candace.

"Hello." replies Jada and Troy.

"Sweetheart, this is Jada and Troy. This is my wife Candace."

"Hello, says Jada. Pleased to meet you. I have heard a lot about you."

"Hello ma'am, it's nice to meet you." says Troy.

"It is a pleasure meeting you both. Please, Troy have a seat." says Candace.

Candace joins them on the sofa. They start a conversation about where they lived. Jada says she likes Candace's home. Next, they get into Jada's job. Candace and DJ let her know how proud they are of her becoming partner in the law ferm.

Candace excuses herself after about 30 minutes to take the casserole out of the oven. She calls the boys into the living room while the bread is baking and introduced them to Jada and Troy. They are very cordial and polite. Traci is all smiles but Kevin on the other hand looks a little confused.

Jada picks up on his confusion then ask him a question that no one expected her to asked.

"Kevin, can we go somewhere so we can talk? If it's okay with your parents?"

"Sure, why not."

"Is it okay DJ, Candace?"

"Sure." they say in unison.

Jada and Kevin go to the Family Room to talk. She explains everything to him. She tells him how she loves him and getting to know him is a dream she has always had. She also hopes he feels the same way. She tells him she wants to be a sister to him and hopes they can be a family.

Kevin looks at her and agrees with her, then tells her he's sorry for being so juvenile and he loves her too. He gives her a big smile, they hug each other then join the others in the Living Room.

"Is everything okay?" asked Candace.

"Yes it is. Everything is just great. Isn't it Kevin?"

"Yes Jada. It is."

He kisses Jada on the cheek and they smile at each other as they look into each others eyes.There is a relationship growing here that not even Jada and Kevin know about.

Candace finally calls everyone to the Dinning Room for dinner and they run over each other trying to get to the table. Candace asked Jada if she would bless the food, and she so graciously accepts and they ate and had a beautiful time as a family.

God has a plan for our lives and we never know what that plan is. We only have to let him lead us and order our steps to see the best way to go. Jada finally found her father and she got a bonus. She got a family that accepts her and will love her unconditionally.

CHAPTER VIII

Prov. 18:22
"Whoso findeth a wife findeth a good thing,
And obtaineth favor of the LORD."

One Plus One Equals One

$\mathcal{A}$ year has come and gone and Jada and her new family are doing just fine and she and Troy are closer than ever. They are all planning a cruise to Jamaica for the summer, which is in two weeks. They are so excited because this is their first trip together since they have gotten together as a family. They have really accepted Jada into the family and the boys are really happy to have a big sister, and believe it or not, they are real protective of her, so Troy has to be on his P's and Q"s.

Vacation day has finally come and all of them are excited to go on the cruise. It's 5:00 AM and Jada's alarm is going off. Her phone rings while she is on her way to the bathroom and it's Troy.

"Hi Babe. It's 5:15 AM and time for you to get up."

"Thanks a lot for calling Sweetie, but I'm already up."

"Okay, I'll pick you up about 8:15 AM. Is that okay?"

"Sure Troy, I'll be waiting."

Jada goes into the shower and her phone rings just as she gets out, it's DJ.

"Hi Baby! Are you up yet?"

"Yes dad, I am. I just got out of the shower."

"Okay, I will see you later. Is Troy picking you up or do you need me to grab you?"

"No dad, Troy is picking me up."

"Okay, see you later."

Troy arrives at Jada's as planned and loads her luggage into the car. They have time for a little breakfast that she has prepared for them. After they eat, they throw the dishes in the dish washer and are on their way.

They meet up with DJ and the others at the Airport. They are going to fly to Florida to their port of call where they will board their ship, "THE BIBLE". What a coincidence that they will be on a ship with a name such as that. This has got to be a great cruise.

"Jada"

Jada remembers and tells them about her Great-Great-Grand Father telling her how his mother and father met on a cruise and they were never happier. As a matter of fact, they made a cruise a wedding gift to everyone in the family who got married.

He told Jada they were such an inspiration and a true example of Unconditional Love to him. Jada wants a love like that when she gets married again. But she knows it will only happen if she allows God to choose for her. So for this reason, she will wait on God's timing and God's choice.

They board the ship and everyone gpes to their own cabins. Jada's cabin is beside Troy's and he is beside the boys. After they get settled in they will all meet on deck to grab a bite to eat.

Food is everywhere. Anything you want is available. They ate and played games and just enjoyed each other.

They sat on deck while they were waiting for the shows to start. Jada and Troy are sitting and talking when a beautiful woman walks over and sits down on the chair beside Troy.

"Well…hellooo handsome!" she says."

"Ooooh…hello." says Troy.

"My name is Summer. What's yours?"

"Troy, and this is a….a…..a…

"Jada! My name is Jada!"

"Hi, nice to meet you both."

"Where are you guys from?"

"We are from Georgia!" said Jada.

"Where are you from?!"

"Oh, I'm from LA."

"Tell me Troy, have you ever been to LA?"

"Yes, I have."

"EXCUSE ME! DO YOU MIND! WE ARE HAVING A CONVERSATION HERE AND YOU AREN"T INVITED!" said Jada with anger in her voice.

"Well excuse me! I was only trying to be friendly."

"BE FRIENDLY SOMEWHERE ELSE, OR FIND YOURSELF FLOATING IN THE OCEAN! HOW ABOUT THAT!!"

Ms. Summer decides she should get her chair and move somewhere else. It might be a bit safer for her.

"Jada, calm down!" said Troy.

"NO TROY, I WON'T CALM DOWN! THIS BIMBO COMES OVER HERE AND DISRESPESCTS ME AND STARTS FLIRTING WITH YOU RIGHT IN FRONT OF ME AND YOU GO ALONG WITH IT. NOW YOU TELL ME TO CALM DOWN! YOU GOT SOME NERVE! AND

SHE DEFINITELY HAS SOME NERVE! SHE DOESN'T KNOW WHO SHE IS COMING UP AGAINST! SHE BETTER ASK SOMEBODY!!"

"Jada, come on, I did nothing wrong!"

"TROY YOU FELL RIGHT INTO THAT TRAP! GET AWAY FROM ME! I WANT TO BE ALONE!"

"Jada!!!"

"LEAVE ME ALONE TROY!!!"

Troy leaves Jada alone and walks around the ship and runs into DJ at the bar. DJ knows something is wrong and invites him to come and join him.

"Troy, what's bothering you son?"

"Your daughter."

"Jada!?"

"Yes, Jada! We were sitting on deck and this young lady comes over, sits down and starts talking to us. Jada gets upset and threatens to throw the woman in the ocean then tells me off and asks me to leave too."

"What! Jada did that!? Troy, what do you mean she sat down to talk to us? Don't you mean she was talking to you?" DJ starts laughing so hard his stomach starts hurting.

"DJ this isn't funny!"

"Troy, Calm down! Jada reminds me of her mother. She is sweet but don't make her mad or she'll be something to deal with. She will be okay Troy, just wait it out and let her cool down. And by the way, look and see if you see any bodies floating in the ocean." He laughs as Troy walks away. Troy looks back at DJ and just shakes his head. He doesn't know what to think. DJ is laughing at a situation that really has him upset.

He doesn't know what Jada is going to do because they have never had a blow up like this one. Yes, they had arguments before but not like this. He felt this is the end of their relationship after all these years. Is he going to enjoy the rest of the cruise with her or is it going to be a miserable vacation? All he can do is pray at this point because he knows prayer changes things.

Jada talked to Candace about what happened between her and Troy and how she feels so disrespected about the whole situation.

"Jada, you have to understand the nature of women. You know women will try to get under your skin any way they can. Only the strong survive. They take what they want, no matter who it belongs to or who it hurts. You know it's their code."

"That doesn't mean that Troy has to go along with it! She was feeding his ego and he was eating it up! I won't stand for that Candace. I think it's disrespectful for him to act that way and I won't let him disrespect me! Who does he think he is? RICK FOXX? I DON'T THINK SO"!

"Jada! Shame on you!! You know it isn't that crucial! You know the bible says you havs to forgive to be forgiven! Where is that Unconditional Love you talk so much about!?"

"I don't know Candace. He just made me so angry! I guess I do have to forgive him though. Don't I?"

"Yes you do Jada. You know things like this are going to come up, especially with Troy. He's a very handsome man and women are going to go after him. So you have to get used to that and trust him. He'll do the right thing Jada, because he loves you. He wouldn't hurt you for the world."

"I know you're right Candace, but it really made me angry. I will apologise to him."

They hug each other and Jada goes on her way to look for Troy. She is still angry, but she knows she has to do the right thing. It wasn't Troy's fault that Summer came over to talk to him. It wasn't like he called her over to sit down.

She has to appologis so they can enjoy the rest of their vacation, because being realistic, Troy did nothing wrong.

She doesn't want to ruin it for everyone else either. They will be upset if she and Troy are fighting. That will be a big damper on the whole vacation for everyone.

Jada finds Troy on John 13:34 Deck. What a coincidence. The Lord works in mysterious ways. Jada walks over to Troy, and he looks at her up over his sunglasses. Jada sits down beside him on a bar stool. She orders a cheeseburger and a coke and looks at him and says:

"Troy, I am so sorry. I was wrong. I shouldn't have blamed you for that fiasco. It wasn't your fault at all. I am truly sorry. Can you forgive me? Please? I am so sorry!"

"Jada, I am so hurt that you would think I would even want anyone else. Especially disrespect you to your face. You know I would never do anything like that! I would leave you before I would hurt you like that. You know I love you. Because I love you, I do forgive you. But, I want you to forgive me too. I didn't handle the situation right. I am so sorry Jada."

"Troy, you have nothing to appologise for. But, thank you anyway and I love you too."

"Are we okay now Jada?"

"Yes Troy, we are. I will never let anything like this happen again. I love you and trust your love for me. I promise I will never do that again."

"I know that Jada. We all make mistakes and misjudge people sometimes. We aren't perfect. As long as you remember that, we will be okay."

They ate their food and went to find the others. They found everyone on "Romans 8:9 Deck". They were getting ready to play "Charades", so they are right on time for the fun.

They are all so glad that Troy and Jada are speaking again. Now they can do what they all came to do....HAVE FUN!!!

CHAPTER IX

Prov. 1:8
"My son, hear the instruction of thy father,
And forsake not the law of thy mother."

Shocking Discovery

*E*verything is getting back to normal after the cruise and everyone had a memorable time. At this point, their plans are to go on a family cruise every year. They are starting a new tradition in the family along with everything else they do. Jada just hasn't told them about all of the traditions in her family yet. Wait until they hear about her traditions when she and Troy get married, they will love them.

Her Great-Great-Grand-Father told her about the traditions in her family and so did her Uncles, so she knows what to do. Actually, she is excited to get started; she can't wait to get married. She and Troy haven't set a date yet but it won't be long now. Cruises do something to people, if you know what I mean.

Jada is having a normal day at work, so she thinks. She then gets a call from Mr. Dent to come to his office. "Jada, I have some bad news for you."

"Mr Dent, I don't need this todaaaay. What now?"

"Do you remember the 12 year old boy you defended about 8 years ago? I think his name is Donnavon Black?"

"Yes, Mr Dent. I remember him very well. Why?"

"Well Jada, he was found slumped down in his car on the interstate last night. They say it is a heart attack. You know his mother was killed in a car wreck when he was five years old and he never knew who his father was. He asked his adoptive mother to call you.

Donnavon is in critical condition and he has asked for you. So, the nurse called me to find you. She says she has tried to call you and keeps getting your voice mail. She has left messages though. I gave her your cell number and sje will call you back in about an hour. I hope that is okay?"

"Oh yes! That is okay. Did she say what his prognosis is? Is he going to be okay?"

"They didn't tell me all of that Jada. I think they want to talk to you about that."

"Okay, thanks Mr. Dent." Jada leaves Mr. Dent's office and goes to her office to wait on the nurse's call. She is worried about Donnavan and also curious about what he wants with her. She and Donnavon have developed a relationship that they never expected would have occurred.

Jada checks her schedule for the day when her phone rings. It is the nurse about Donnavan. She tells Jada that Donnavon wants her to come to the hospital so they can talk. He has something very important he needs to talk to her about and can't do it on the phone. Jada tells the nurse to tell Donnavon she will be there in the morning.

She finishes her day, but still wonders what Donnavon has to talk to her about. When she gets home, she calls Troy to let him know she is going to New York to meet with Donnavon. She decides to leave that night instead of waiting until morning. Troy insists on going with her. He meets her at her house to pick her up and they head to the airport.

Once they arrived at the airport in NY they get the hotel shuttle to their hotel. They check into their rooms, get settled in, and go out to have a late dinner.

Jada tosses and turnes all night wondering what is wrong with Donavon. She has a strange feeling about this meeting and can't put it out of her mind so she can rest. She does know though, that God is going to make everything alright if they just leave it all up to him. So that's what she decides to do.

The following morning, Troy rents a car and he and Jada head to the hospital to meet with Donnavon. Once they arrive at the hospital, Troy waits in the waiting room while Jada goes in to talk with Donnavon.

Jada walks over to Donnavon's bed and he is lying so still. He has tubes and wires going everywhere and he looks so helpless lying there. She takes his hand and calls his name:

"Donnavon, Donnavon, it's Jada. I'm here Donnavon. Can you open your eyes and talk to me?"

Donnavon opens his eyes, and in a very weak voice he says: "Jada, I knew you would come. Thank you so much."

"You know I would never let you down Sweetie. I love you and I always will. Donnavan, what do you want to talk to me about?"

"Jada, my adoptive mother told me who my real father is and I want you to try to find him for me. Can you do that for me?"

"Yes Donnavon, anything for you. What is his name? Do you know where he lives? Can you give me all the information that you have?"

Shocking Discovery

"His name is Dana Jordan, but people call him DJ. She says she thinks he lives in Georgia somewhere. Jada, can you find him? PLEASE JADA!?"

Jada stands there with her mouth open and doesn't know what to say. She does know she has to say something though. She gets herself together and looks him in his eyes and said:

"Donnavon, I will do my best to find him for you. You can believe that. I have to go now, but I will be back this evening. I love you Donnavon. You get some rest."

Donnavon closes his eyes and falls off to sleep.

Jada turns and slowly walks out of Donnavon's room, trying to put the pieces together of what he has told her. She closes the door quietly and starts down the hall with a questioning look on her face. She didn't know what to do now.

As she gets closer to where Troy is sitting her legs get weaker and weaker. As she approaches the chair her legs are gone and Troy has to jump up and catch her to keep her from hitting the floor.

"Jada! What's wrong! What happened?"

"Troy, I can't believe what just happened. Donnavon wants me to help him find his father."

"Well Jada, you can do that. What's the problem?!"

"Troy! His father is DJ! Dana Jordan! My father is Donnavon's father! Donnavan is my brother Troy! What am I going to do? How am I going to tell him that I'm his sister? What am I going to tell DJ and Candace and the boys? I don't know what to do Troy!"

Jada is estactic. She finds out that the young boy she defended in a murder trial, years ago is her little brother. She is so disturbed about this new information. She is shocked, not angry that she has received the news she has received. She knows now why the bond she feels for Donnavan is so strong.

She knows there is a tie between them but she couldn't put her finger on it. She now has the missing piece of the puzzle....maybe? She just has to figure out how to put it into place. She is going to affect so many lives with the information she has to deliver.

CHAPTER X

Luke 12:2
*"For there is nothing covered, that shall not be revealed;
Neither hid, that shall not be known."*

The Reveal

*J*ada is walking the floor all night trying to figure out how she is going to break the news to DJ and the rest of the family. How can she tell them the news she has just found out.

She especially doesn't know how Dana is going to take it. This is the same young man that was on trial for attacking him and killing his friend, although he was innocent, he was still there.

"My God, how am I going to break the news to my family about Donnavan? You have to give me the words to say God. I am at a loss. I don't want to hurt anyone and yet, it has to be told. Please help me God! I know I can do all things with your help".

With tears streaming down her face, Jada continues to talk to God and ask him for guidance. She finally gets her answer and settles down to try and get a couple of hours of sleep before she has to make that drive to Dana's house and break the news to them.

Morning finally comes and Jada starts her morning. She is so glad it's a weekend so she doesn't have to worry about going in to work with all of this on her mind. She stops on her way out the door to call Troy to ask him to meet her at Dana's for a little moral support.

Jada and Troy arrive at Dana's about the same time. Jada tells Dana she has something important to tell them. Dana gathers everyone together in the den and gives Jada the floor. Jada feels a calm come over her as Troy speaks up.

"Go on Babe. It's okay. You can do this. I am right here."

"Dana...everyone.....I have something to tell you. Dana, do you remember the young man that was accused of attacking you, but was found innocent of the whole crime?"

"Yes Jada. His name is uuuh....Donald, Douglas or something like that."

"His name is Donnavan, Dana."

The Reveal

"Yes! That's it, Donnavan! What about him?"

"Well Dana....it turns out that that young man, Donnavan is......"

"Is what Jada?"

"He is your son Dana."

Everything and everyone is silent. You can hear a pin drop. Dana's mouth falls open and everyone has a look of total shock on their face.

"Dana are you okay?"

"Hooow did you find this out Jada? Are you sure? Where is he?"

"Yes Dana. I am sure. He is in the hospital. He sent for me and ask me to help him find his father. All evidence leads to you Dana. You're his father. The paramedics found him in his car after having a heart attack. He has no other immediate family except us Dana. What are you going to do now that you know the truth?"

"Jada, I don't know what to do. I am in shock. Who is his mother? I....I......Jada, I just don't know what to do."

"Candace?"asked Jada, have you taken this all in?"

"Yes, Jada, I have. I am very shocked that my husband has has such a checkered past! Dana! Are there any more children out there that I don't know about?!"

Dana looked at her with tear filled eyes and said:

"Candace, that isn't fair. I didn't know about Donnavan. I would have told you if I did. I told you about Jada when I found out about her. I would never keep something like this from you. You know that. I love you too much. I wouldn't do anything to make you leave me or hate me. Please understand Candace, I wouldn't do anything to hurt you and the boys, and Jada either. They say that your past will catch up with you but this is a past that I didn't know anything about. Please Candace, believe me!"

"I believe you Dana, but it doesn't make it any better. I don't hate you. I love you too much and I always will. UNCONDITIONALLY! What are we going to do? Boys what do you think?"

The boys look at each other and pause until Traci finally speaks up.

"Dad we are family, and family sticks together no matter what. We accept and love Jada like she has always been here and we can do the same for our brother Donnavan."

"Kevin, are you on board with your brother?"

"Yes, dad, 100% on board."

"Candace, it's up to you now. What do you say we do?"

The Reveal

Candace looks around the room at everyone and tears fall down her cheeks like she has just been slapped. She walks over to Dana, stands before him and kneels down. She takes his hands and says;

"Dana, Sweetheart……, I will do the right thing. I don't want to hurt anyone and don't want God to be angry with me. I think you should go see your son and see what he has to say about things. If he wants to be a part of this family, then we welcome him with open arms. We will love him forever and that is a promise."

Dana bends down, pulls Candace to her feet and hugs her with tears running down his face. The boys and Candace join in the group hug.

The following day, Jada calls Donnavan to make arrangements to see him. What he doessn't know is, she is bringing his father with her.

When Jada, Dana, and Troy arrive at the hospital the next day, Donovan is so glad to see them. She introduces him to Troy and then tells him she has something to talk to him about.

"Donnavan, I searched for your father and I did find him. He lives in Georgia. He is married and has two boys, Traci and Kevin. His wife's name is Candace. Your father's name is Dana, as you already know, they call him DJ."

"Jada, what is he like? Did you tell him about me? Does he want to meet me? What did he say"?

"He is a very nice man Donnavan and his family is nice too. I told him everything about you and he wants to meet you."

"When am I going to meet him Jada?"

"How about now Donnavan?"

"He's here!? My father is here?! Where is he Jada?!"

"He's outside in the lobby. Do you want me to get him?"

"Yes! Please!"

Jada goes out to get DJ to bring him in to meet Donovan. What a surprise for Donovan when DJ walks into the room.

"It's....It's......It's...you!"

Donovan remembered the man from the courtroom and was very surprised.

"Don't worry Donnavan. It's okay. All is forgotten and forgiven. My name is Dana....I'm your father. I'm sorry I didn't know you before now and missed so much of your life. But, I didn't know about you, and I am sorry for that."

"That wasn't your fault Dana. You can't be blamed for something you didn't know about. You can only correct it when you find out about it. I hold no grudges against you for the past. I want to apologise to you for the assault. I had no idea what was going on until it all went down. I was with

The Reveal

the wrong people and I learned a lesson from it all. Please forgive me."

"Son...I forgave you long ago. Now you need to forget about It and forgive yourself. Let's put all of that behind us and start fresh. How does that work for you? Is that okay?"

"Sure Dana. That works for me. Thank you Jada for finding my father for me."

"You are so welcome Donnavan, but there is something else you need to know."

"What is that Jada?"

"Donnavan, Dana is also my father. I am your sister."

"WHAT! I don't believe this. How could this be? We are family? You're my sister?" I couldn't be happier Jada."

"Me either Donnavan, me either."

They all hug each other and leave the hospital so Donnavan can get some rest. They tell him they will be back later to check on him and talk to the doctor about moving him to a hospital in Georgia so they can be closer to him, take care of him, and get to know each other better.

The news is all so exciting and surprising and they are going to make it all work for their good.

After a few weeks Donnavan is out of the hospital and staying with DJ until they can find him a house of his own.

They aren't rushing the issue because they want to make sure he is well enough to be on his own.

The boys enjoy having him around so much. The big brother they never had and always wanted is finally here and they love every minute of it. Donnavon takes on the position like he hads always been here and he loves the boys with all his heart.

He didn't know what he had been missing until he met all of them. His family is a blessing in disguise and he feels he is so blessed to have them.

CHAPTER XI

Mathew 21:22
"And all things, whatsoever ye shall ask in prayer, believing, ye shall receive."

A New Life

DJ finds Donnavon a house three houses down the street from he lives and he hopes Donnavon will like it. He rushes home to tell Donnavon what he has found. Donnavon says he doesn't want to live that close to his family and wants a house farther away.

DJ is heart broken and his face drops so that he looks like a bull dog. Donnavon looks at him and says:

"DJ, I'm only kidding."

He laughs so hard at DJ that he cries.

DJ promises him he will get him back for that one. He says that is so wrong and he has a good one coming.

"Donnavon, you got me this time. I really thought you were serious about not wanting to live close to us. Do you want to go see it? If you like it we will put a bid in on it."

"Sure, I would love to."

"Great! I will call and see if we can look at it in the morning."

DJ makes the call and they have an appointment to go see the house now if they like.

"We can go now if you likd Donnavon."

"Sure DJ, lets go."

DJ and Donnavon go look at the house and Donnavon loves it. They put their bid in on the house and two days later they get a call that the house is his if he wants it. Donnavon is estatic and can't wait to move into it.

The next couple of days the whole family gets together to help Donnavon move into his new home. He decides to have the kitchen remolded. He buys a new living room suit but, everything else he purchased before going into the hospital.

Everyone is working so hard at getting Donnavon moved into his new home. Everything is finally done and it is time for everyone to take a break and settle down a bit.

DJ decides to order Chinese food for dinner and the ladies get the table cleared so they can enjoy a first meal in Dannavon's new home.

After dinner Donnavon turnes, the TV on for the kids in the family room and turns on some music for the adults in the living room. They are enjoying themselves talking, joking and telling stories, or should I say telling lies. But, they are having a real nice time doing nothing but enjoying each other and making plans for the future.

Donnavon tells DJ that family is the way to go and the love they show is all he needs to survive. Jada speaks up and says:

"Family love is nice but you better lean on God's love. That's how you survive. You can't make it without Him."

"I know that. That's a fact. But I don't mean it that way. I know God has my back when no one else does. That isn't even up for debate." says Donnavon.

Everyone starts to settle down so they can get ready for church the next day. Jada is going to have to be there early because she is in the choir and they have to get ready for a big concert.

They all start to file out one by one to go home. They are in walking distance so no one has to drive home. Donnavon

"Jada"

walks Jada home because she is going in the opposite direction from everyone else. On the way home they run into Pryce. Pryce is a very good and old friend of Jada's.

"Hi Jada!"

"Well, hello Pryce! Pryce, this is my borther Donnavon. Donovan this is Pryce. Pryce is a real good friend of mine."

"Hello Pryce! It is nice to meet you."

"You too Donnavon."

"Jada, I didn't know you had a brother,especially one so handsome."

"Oh my goodness! Thank you Pryce. That is very kind of you and you are a Beautiful Lady too." says Donovan.

Jada laughs at both of them as they make googly eyes at each other and trade smiles.

"Come on you two, this is getting to be too much."

She laughed at them both and shakes her head.

"Donnavon and I as brother and sister is a long story Pryce, but I'll tell you all about it tomorrow. I will see you at church, okay?"

"Maybe you can go to dinner with us after church Pryce?" interjected Donnavon.

"Oh, I would love to Donnavon, if it's okay with Jada and the rest of the family."

A New Life

"You know you are always welcome Pryce. See you in the morning."

"See you Jada. Oh! See you tomorrow too Donnavon and you have a good night."

"You too Pryce. Be careful going home. Do you need an escort?"

"Thanks! I will. And no Donnavon. I will be okay. It's only a block down the street and it's very well lit. Thank you anyway."

"No problem. Have a good night." said Donnavon.

Sunday morning couldn't come fast enough for Donnavon. He is so excited about seeing Pryce he can't sleep.

All of the family meets up at Donnavon's house so they can go to church together. This is the first Sunday that Donnavon is going to church with the rest of the family.

When they arrive at church, Pryce is the first person they see. It is like she is hovering like a buzzard waiting for them to show up. Or should I say waiting for Donnavon to show up.

When they arrive at church, Donnavon walks up to Pryce and greets her with a little hug. The rest of the family looks at them like,.....what is going on here?? Jada explains how they ran into Pryce when Donnavon was walking her home Saturday night.

"Jada"

After church, they decide to go to "The Palace" for dinner. The Palace has the best food in town. It is a little expensive, but the food is great so it is worth every penny. They serve that good old Southern Cooking like Grandma used to cook. They don't mind splurging for Donovan this one time. Who knows, his relationship with Pryce could turn out to be something.

All of them hope the relationship grows because Pryce has been around the family every since Jada was in grade school. She is like famil to everyone but Donnavon. Pryce is a real nice girl and will be really good for Donnavon and he will be good for her too.

After dinner they all go to DJ's house to relax and enjoy each others company. They even play some spades and the kids play board games. The kids favorite game is "Don't Break The Ice and Operation." The older kids are playing video games and Monopoly. What it all boils down to is that everyone is doing their own thing and having a great time.

The evening is winding down and Donnavon is the first one to leave because he has to get up earlier than usual Monday morning to go in to work. He has a client coming in that he has made special arrangements for.

A New Life

Pryce stops him as he is leaving and ask if she can walk with him. He is more than happy to have her company. As they leave, everyone teases them just like family does.

YOU GOT TO LOVE THEM!! FAMILY IS ALL YOU HAVE!

CHAPTER XII

1 Thessalonians 3:8
"For now we live, if ye stand fast in the Lord."

Favor Is Forever

As the months go by, Donnavon and Pryce become more close. Donnavon wants to ask Pryce to marry him but he doesn't think she will because of his tainted past. Although he is saved now and truly grounded in the Lord and doesn't live that life anymore, he still doubts that she will have someone like him for the rest of her life. And, because they have only know each other for about 10 month. He thinks she won't think that is long enough to start talking about marriage.

What will he do? Will he muster up the nerve to ask her and find out what the outcome will be? He doesn't know what to do so he comes up with the idea to call Jada and talk to her about it. After all, Pryce is her best friend. She will know how Pryce will feel about the relationship being so new. He really loves Pryce and only hopes and prays that she feels the same way about him.

Donnavon goes into the kitchen and makes himself a sandwich and gets a glass of milk, siits down, and calls Jada. The phone rings about seven times. Just as he is aboutto hang up Jada answers the phone.

"Hello."

"Jada! I was getting ready to hang up. I thought you were asleep."

"No Sweetie, I was in the shower. What's up?"

"Hon, I need to talk to you about Pryce."

"Oh my God! What happen?!"

"Oh! No! No! Nothing Happened! Everything is okay. I just wantto get your advice on something. That's all."

"Oh, okay! What can I help you with?"

"Well Jada, you know Pryce and I haven't bee together long, but I really love her."

"Oh that is so sweet Donnavon. Go on".

"I can only hope that she feels the same way about me."

"I know she does Don."

"Really?! Well, this is the issue. Don't say anything Jada until I am finished. Like I said..... I really love her and I want to ask her to marry me but I don't know what she will say, because we haven't been together long. What do you think Jada? Should I ask her or should I wait?"

"Donnavon! That is so wonderful! No, don't wait! Ask her! Ask her tonight! Don't wait Don, I know what she will say!"

"Are you sure Jada?"

"Yes Don, I am sure, ask her!"

"Okay Sweetie, I will. Thanks Jada. I love you."

You are welcome Honey! I am so happy for you Don, you couldn't have made a better choice. The two of you will be good together. Let God lead you in what to say and how to ask and it will come out okay."

"Okay Jada I will. Thanks, and have a good evening."

"You too Don. Talk to you later. Goodbye."

The following day wasn't an easy one for Donnavon, He is so nervous about what to say to Pryce and what she would say back to him. He loves her so much and wants to spend the rest of his life with her. He has never loved anyone like this before. He has truly found his soul mate and hopes and prays that she has also found hers in him.

Donnavon has a rough day at work and decides to call Pryce to ask her to go to a movie so he can calm down a bit. After the movie they go to Jay's Soda Shop that is just a block from his house. He just wants to get out and relax for a while, nothing special…..so he thinks.

When he gets home there are candles lit, music playing, dinner in the oven, and a box of purple long stem roses for Pryce on the living room table. And on the end table by the love seat,. a bottle of chilled non-alcoholic champagne and chocolate dipped strawberries. There is a note in an envelope with Donnavon's name on it leaning against the champagne bucket and it reads:

"DONNAVON, THIS IS HOW WE DO THINGS"
GOOD LUCK! WE LOVE YOU!
YOUR SIBLINGS

Donnavon is outdone, he doesn't know what to think. He is really nervous now. He has never had anyone do something so nice for him, and he is almost in tears. He doesn't let Pryce in on the antics yet, but he will later. She thinks he set this whole scene up.

As the evening goes on Donnavon becaomes more relaxed and decides it is time to pop the question. Donnavon sits down beside Pryce on the love seat and takes the glass out of her hand and sits it on the table. He looks her in her eyes and says:

"Pryce you know I love you very much don't you?"

"Yes Donnavon I do. What's wrong?!"

"Nothing is wrong Sweetheart. I just want you to know how much I love you and I always will. I love you more that anything, and I want to be with you for the rest of my life. Will you do me the honor of being my wife? Marry me? Please?"

Donnavon pulls out a box with the most beautiful diamond ring she has ever seen.

"Donnavon! You want me to marry you?!"

"Yes I do Pryce. Will you be my wife?"

"Yes Donnavon! Yes! I will be your wife!"

Donnavon places the ring on her ring finger and they kiss and hug each other and laugh the happiest laugh you have ever heard.

They love each other so much that they know this is a love put together by God. A love no man can tear apart.

The two of them talk and finish their dinner before going to see Jada and the rest of the family. They know they areover there waiting for them to bring some good news.

When they get to Jada's, Donnavon rings the door bell and goes in first and alone while Pryce hides behind the trees in the yard. Jada answers the door with a big smile until she sees Donnavon standing alone with a sad look on his face. She looks at him and places her hand over her mouth and says;

"OH NO! DONNAVON! SHE SAID NO!! I CAN'T BELIEVE IT! I TRULY THOUGHT SHE WAS GOING TO SAY YES! I THOUGHT SHE REALLY LOVED YOU ENOUGH TO MARRY YOU! I HONESTLY DID! HONEY, I AM SO SORRY!"

"Jada, sometimes we just don't know people like we think we do."

"Come in Donnavon. I am so sorry! I really am. So sorry. I know how much you love her."

"It's okay Jada."

While they are telling the others what is going on the door bell rings. When Jada answered the door there stands Pryce with a sad look on her face.

"Why are you looking so sad Pryce?" asked Jada.

"You haven't heard Jada?"

"What Pryce?"

"Donnavon asked me to marry him tonight."

"Come in Pryce. The rest of the family is in the living room. I am sure they will love to hear what you have to say."

They walk into the living room and she says hello to everyone and sees Donnavon sitting in the corner of the room.

"Oh, hello Donnavon. I didn't know you were here."

"Hello Pryce."

"I'm sure you didn't said Jada."

"Donnavon did you tell them the news?"

"You can tell them your version Pryce."

"As I was telling Jada.... Donnavon asked me to marry him tonight and, well.........

"Well what Pryce?" interupted Jada.

"Well....I said.......YES!"

Then she showed them the ring.

"DONNAVON!!!!! HOW COULD YOU DO THIS TO US?!! YOU SHOULD BE ASHAMED OF YOURSELF!"

Jada picks up a pillow from the sofa and starts hitting him with it. Pryce jumps in to stop her and Jada starts hitting her too. It turns into a big pillow fight and free for all. But, it's a lot of fun.

CHAPTER XIII

Psalms 27:14
"Wait on the Lord: be of good courage, and he shall strengthen thine heart: wait, I say, on the Lord."

LOVE PREVAILES

Everyone is still rejoicing over the engagement of Pryce and Donnavon. But what they don't know is......Jada and Troy are making wedding plans too. They started to announce their engagement when Donnavon asked Jada for help with asking Pryce about marrying him. For this reason, Jada and Troy decide to put their announcement on hold until Pryce and Donnavon get their wedding out of the way. This doesn't quite work though because Donnavon finds out about their engagement and confronts Jada about it.

"Jada, I hear you and Troy are engaged to be married and aren't telling anyone about it. Well you guys are going to tell the family tonight and that is final. And I talked to Pryce and we want you to have a double wedding with us. And, we won't take no for an answer."

"No Donnavon! I don't want to take away from Pryce's day."

"JADA!!!!! IF YOU DON'T......WE DON'T! JUST AS SIMPLE AS THAT! SO WHAT'S IT GONNA BE? IS THERE GOING TO BE A WEDDING ON NO WEDDING? IT'S YOUR CALL?"

"Let me talk to Troy about it and I will let you know."

"And the same goes for him too. If he doesn't no one does. Won't be any wedding. Pryce and I have already made that decision."

"Oooooh, Donnavon, I love you so much. Nobody can ask for a better brother."

"Wellllll.....they could.....but, they wouldn't get one."

They hug each other and laugh a big hearty laugh as they walk to Donnavon's house.

That evening when Troy gets back in town, Jada talks to him about Donnavon and Pryce's plans about a double wedding. He feels the same way Jada does about it. But when she tells him all of the plans, just like Jada, he has no choice but to agree.

They call Donnavon to let him know it is a go. They will give in to his and Pryce's blackmail. They all laugh about it and it is going to be a great occasion.

The following evening after everyone gets off work, the four of them call everyone over to Jada's house. They have hor'douvres and coffee set for them.

"What's going on ask DJ?"

"We just want to let you all know that Troy and I are getting married." Said Jada.

"And we are having a double wedding." adds Donnavon.

Everyone is so happy about the weddings. They are estatic about planning for everything. They do have Jada's Grandfather Rick performing the wedding. And Rick has a surprise psalmist that is coming with him to sing at the wedding. Pryce had already gotten in touch with him so that was in stone.

Jada and Pryce go out shopping for wedding gowns and Candace and the rest of the ladies go with them. Since Pryce and Jada are the brides, Candace is going to be Jada's Maid of Honor and Danai is going to be Pryce's. DJ is going to give Jada away and Da`jour, Jada's cousin is going to give Pryce away.

The girls go to every Bridal Shop in town and end up going back to the first one that started the journey. Jada finds a beautiful strapless gown with pearls lining the bustline and down the long sleeves and outlining the train.

Pryce on the other hand finds a gown with one lace sleeve and the other sleeveless. It has a see through bodice and pearls lining her train also. Both gowns are beautiful.

After they purchase their gowns, they go home and sit in the den to go over the specifics of the wedding. They decide the colors will be purple and white and of course Jada's Grandfather, Rick, is doing the crermony.

They make an invitation list, get the decorating committee organized, contact the caterers, and get the Rotunda at the Capitol for the ceremony. They are going to have their reception at the Embassy Suites due to the number of people that will be attending.

They finally get all of their wedding plans together, all of the invitations sent out, and the date is February 14. They think it will be a great day to be married. The perfect day for love. They also make plans to honeymoon in Jamaica for a week.

Everything is in order and everyone is doing their job as directed. Everything is falling into place like a jigsaw puzzle.

Love Prevailes

Things are too good to be true, but, it is all true. They are all so happy and they are getting married in a couple of weeks. They are busy but they enjoy every minute of it. Like they say....there is nothing like family.

They can't wait to see what Grandpa Rick has planned for them, and who this great Psalmist is he is bringing with him. It is all so exciting and everyone is about to POP!

The days are winding down. They are down to the last days. Troy and Donnavon go to the airport to pick Rick and his surprise Psalmist up. Everyone is so excited, they can't wait until they get back from the airport.

They hear the car drive into the garage. They rise to their feet and turn towards the sound. Rick walks in with the guys and hugs everyone with the biggest smile on his face. Jada looks at him and asks:

"Grandpa? Where is the surprise?"

He looks at her and turns her towards the door. In the doorway stands Jason, Angelo, Casey, and Jason Angelo.

"OH MY GOD! I AM NOT SEEING THIS! THIS CAN'T BE HAPPENING! ARE YOU ALL REALLY HERE?!"

Jason speaks up, as uaual, and says:

"Jada"

"Yes sweetie, we are really here. We wouldn't miss this wedding for the world. You know we love you. Our baby cousins are getting married. Yes Pryce.... you are family too."

"Wait a minute! Where are your wives?"

"Don't worry, said Casey. They will be here tomorrow. They have to spend some more money and do some last minute things for you guys."

Everyone starts laughing then they sit down and enjoy the rest of the evening. What Pryce and Jada don't know is that the wives were already in town. They are preparing a surprise bridal shower for the two ladies at the Embassy Suites and they are going to spend the night there getting things prepared for the following day.

The next morning, everyone gets up early to get the day started. Casey takes Pryce and Jada down town to do their last minute shopping and last minute pickups.

They pick up their gowns and shoes; check on the flowers and cake; and make sure the venue was secure.

They don't have any Brides Maides because their families are so far away. So, they are going to just use Maids of Honor. So they thought. What they don't know is, Bethany, Nevaeh, Danni, and Bonnie are going to be Brides Maids for them.

Dannai's Great-granddaughters Rain and Blythe are going to be the Flower Girls. Nevaeh's Grandsons Jacari and Cameron are going to be the Ring Bearers.

They have Angelo and Jason as the Best Men and Angelo, Jason, Casey and Jason Angelo as the Groomsmen. And yes, you guessed it, Jason is the Psalmist for the wedding.

Danai was on the phone with Candace the whole time helping make these arrangements for them and they are really going to be surprised.

Casey takes Pryce and Jada back home so they can rest a little before they all go out to dinner because he has to go to the airport to pick up their wives on the way. At least this is what Jada and Pryce think.

Jason, being the voice of everyone as usuall, standa up and says:

"Come on you guys, it's time to go. We have reservation for dinner and we have to pick the girls up at the airport too. Let's get a move on."

Everyone loads up in the cars and heads out. Jason asks to stop at the Embassy Suites to make sure everything is straight for the reception. As he gets out of the car, he turns and tells Jada and Pryce to go with him to make sure everything is correct.

After they get in the hotel, everybody else starts getting out of the cars and running in the side door. Jason asks the clerk if he can see the room where the reception will be held. He proceeds to take them to the room. When they walk into the room everyone yells:

"SURPRISE!"

Jada and Pryce are really surprised. They are happy to see the girls too. They yell at Rick and Jason for lying to them about the girls not being in town yet.

Everyone has a great time and they enjoy seeing everybody again. It is always nice seeing family that you love when you haven't seen them in such a long time. It is good talking to them on the phone but it isn't the same as seeing them in person.

CHAPTER XIV

1 Corinthians 13:4-5
"Love is patient, love is kind, it is not envious.Love does not brag, it is not puffed up.It is not rude, it is not self-serving, it is not easily angered or resentful."

Love Everlasting

It's wedding day and everyone is heading to the Capitol to get things underway. They want to do one last check to make sure everything is in order and ready to go. That is, everyone but Jada and Pryce. They aren't allowed to go. You know the old saying. Groom can't see the bride before the wedding.

Casey picks Jada and Pryce up later and takes them to another part of the building where they can get dressed and meet with the other girls.

Rick goes in to talk to Jada and Pryce to let them know that he has another gift for them. He will give it to them at

"Jada"

the reception. In the meantime, Jason is meeting with Troy and Donnovan to tell them the same thing.

The time has come and the men and Rick are heading out to the Rotunda. There are at least 300 or more people there. They had no idea that it would be that many guest.

Jason sends his friend Mason to let the caterers know they need to add more guest to the list. They had only planned for about 200. They have to add the rest of the guest to the list and it is good they planned ahead for the extra, just in case. They did inform the caterers to be on standby just in case more than anticipate show up. That is exactly what happened. But the caterer is on it and is doing a terrific job getting things set up for more.

The procession is getting on the way and the grooms are taking their places. One is on the right and one is on the left. The brides will be in the middle. They are going to have their Brides Maids, Maid of Honors, Groomsmen, Ring Bearers, and the Flower Girls, line up behind theGrooms and Brides on a slant. Sounds like it won't work, but it looks great.

The Brides party starts down the isle while the music is starting to play. The Ring Bearers go down and take their place on both sides of Rick and turn to faced the Grooms. The Flower girls come down the aisle and take their place to the inside of the Grooms. The Groomsmen, escorting the Brides maids, take their places on the outside of the Grooms on a slant.

The doors close and they are awaiting the Brides. The Pianist starts to play "One In A Million" as the Brides, walking side by side with their escorts, start down the aisle led by their Maidof Honors.

Jason starts to sing "One In A Million" then steps aside and Troy takes over. Jada has no idea that Troy can even sing. She is so surprised. The tears roll down her face.

Once the Brides get halfway down the aisle, they stop to let Troy finish the song. But wait, the second verse was handed over to Donnavon. Pryce cried;

"OH MY GOD! I HAD NO IDEA!"

The two ladies stand there with tears running down their cheeks. So much for makup. When the guys finish singing, the music continues to play until the girls make their way to their Grooms.

The wedding is going so beautifully. The couples have even written their own vows. When they recite their vows, there isn't a dry eye in the place, and this includes the Grooms and the Brides. Rick even has tears in his eyes. It is a beautiful moment that will never be forgotten.

After the ceremony the procession walks out to the music of "One In A Million".

The Wedding Party meets in a meeting room at the Capitol to take photos. Then they go outside on the steps to take more. After they finish with the photos, they head to the Embassy Suites for the Reception. When they get there everyone greets them and raises their glasses in a toast to the Newlyweds.

They eat, dance, talk and have a nice time mingling with each other. The time comes to open their gifts. The ladies hand them out in the order they want them to be opened.

After all the gifts are opened, Rick speaks up and says:

"Wait! We have one more gift for you to open."

He hands Troy and Donnavon a small folder trimed in gold with their last name on it. They open it with the wives and start to read. Troy speaks up and says:

"RICK! JASON! GUYS! THIS IS TOO MUCH! ARE YOU GUYS SERIOUS! IS THIS ANOTHER ONE OF YOUR MANY JOKES?"

Donnavon agrees with him.

"No it isn't too much and it isn't a joke. Ask Jada about what you have and she can tell you what is going on here."

"Troy... Donnavon.... this is the way it is. Whenever someone in our family got married, my Great Grandfather

Love Everlasting

Sean always paid for the honeymoon. Before he passed, he asked Jason to keep the tradition going. That's what they are doing here today. If I know Jason and Rick, this isn't the end of Grandpa's tradition. We want to say a "GREAT BIG THANK YOU" from the bottom of our hearts."

"You are truly welcome. Now tell everyone what you are holding in your hands."

"They have given us a two week honeymoon cruise, which includes a week in Hawaii and a week in the Bahamas."

A barrage of cheers and hand claps go out in the room and congradulations follow.

The reception ends and the four of them makes their way to the airport. They are catching their flight to go to their Port of Call so they can board the ship called "The Dream."

Rick has made arrangements ahead of time with their bosses at work. He ask for them to have some extra time off and ask the bosses to promise not to tell them about the arrangements.

Once on board the ship they have ajoining suites with a deck. At night they sit on their decks and talk, looking over the ocean and looking at the sky. It was a beautiful view. Something they will never want to leave or forget.

"Jada"

The food is great and so is the entertainment. They play games and lay out on deck and listen to the music that is playing over the loud speakers.

They night of the Captains Dinner they dress in their formal attire and take pictures before going to their table. There are two seatings just for them which have a dozen roses for Jada and a dozen for Pryce. Of course they are from Rick. After dinner they will be leaving the Bahamas to go to Hawaii.

After a night of cruising, they have finally arrived in Hawaii. Hawaii is so beautiful and a real tropical paradise. They get of the ship in Maui to go do some shopping. They shop for 4 hours before returning to the ship.

After returning to the ship they find candles, candy and more flowers in their cabins. There is also a heart shaped necklace for Jada and Pryce with diamond lining the heart and one purple diamond in the middle. But, that's not all. There are two boxes of chocolate covered strawberries, champagne on ice, and a key in a box that says try me out when you get home.

On one box was the name Mr. and Mrs Mason and on the other box was Mr. and Mrs. Black Both written in gold raised lettering.

This really has them puzzled but they can only wait until they get home to see what it is. The four of them play a guessing game to try to find out what the key goes to. They will just have to wait and see.

The cruise is winding down and they are almost ready to pull into port to head home. Once they dock they have to catch an hour flight home. Although they had a great time on their honeymoon, they are really glad to get back home to see their families and start their new lives together.

CHAPTER XV

Psalms 40:1;5
"I waited patiently for the LORD; and he inclined unto me, and heard my cry.
5a: Many O LORD my God (are) thy wonderful works (which) thou hast done, and thy thoughts (which are) to us-ward: they cannot be reckoned up in order unto thee:"

God's Promises

The Newlyweds make it home and drive into the Blacks drive way to unload the luggage. They help them take their luggage into the foyure, hug them goodby and head home. When they get home they pull into their driveway. The driveway is easier than the garage to unload the luggage and take it into the house.

When they enter the house, Troy's phone rings. It's Donnavon.

"Hey Donnavon. What's up?"

"Troy, when you went into the house did you notice the music playing in the living room?"

"Yes, Donnavon I did. But, it is playing in my bed room too. I don't know what's going on. I will call you back later after I figure this out."

"Okay, later."

Troy sits the luggage down in the foyer and walks into the living room. There is candlelight, champagne, choclate covered strawberries and cherries, whipped cream, a gift for Jada and an envelop for Troy.

"What is this? Jada, what is going on?"

"Open the envelope Troy."

Troy opens the envelope and reads it out loud:

"Congradulations on your beautiful wedding. The love you two share will last forever if you keep God in it. Don't ever go to bed angry with each other. Love you both with an Unconditional Love Always.....

Rick and the Gang."

"I should have known it was them. I forgot how they operate. Troy, this isn't all. There is something else. I don't know what, but there is."

They sit down and enjoy some of the strawberries and stuff left on the table. They then decide to take their bags to the bedroom. Jada takes her gift with her and opens it there. It is of course a beautiful negligee and a bottle of her favorite cologne. On the bed is another envelope. Inside it says:

**Go to the garage and
let us know
what you find and think!**

Troy and Jada look at each other with a puzzled look and head to the garage. There was a new car, a Silver Benz. They are so surprised. Jada starts to cry and Troy takes her in his arms. They go into the house to call Donnavon and Pryce. They have to make sure this isn't all a dream.

"Hello...... Donnavon.... this is Troy. Is there anything strange going on over there?"

"Troy, you won't believe it! There are things all over the house and a Benz in the garage! A GOLD one! Rick and the guys did this and I can't believe it! I am outdone! I don't know what to say! This is too much! I have to go over there and thank them!"

"I know what you mean Donnavon. It is way more than I would have ever expected. Leave your car and I will come and pick you and Pryce up and we will go together. The same thing is going on over here too. I am on my way."

Troy hangs up the phone and he and Jada head over to pick Donnavon and Pryce up. They head to the hotel to meet Rick and the rest of the family. They decided to go there after the wedding to give the newlyweds some alone time. When they arrive at the hotel, Rick is surprised to see them because they have just gotten back from their honeymoon.

"My goodness! Is the honeymoon over all reasy?! Is something wrong and you guys already need counceling?"

Rick laughs and invites them in. The ladies are the first into the room to hug Rick. Then they make their way around the room to everyone else, with the men following behind them. Donnavon speaks up:

"Pryce and I want to thank you from the botton of our hearts for everything you've done for us. We truly appreciate it and you have done too much. God knows you have."

"We do too.. We don't know how to thank you. We can't thank you enough. Like Donnavon says, you have really done too much." says Troy.

"No, we haven't, and we don't need any thanks. We do it because we love you, UNCONDITIONALLY. This will never change, no matter what. We want to do it. It has always been a tradition in our family and when we are gone, please promise us you will continue to carry it on. It was handed down to us from our Great-Grandparents, Sean and Stephanie, and we have kept it going. So we want to ask you to do the same. Promise us."

"We promise we will", says the four of them.

"As time goes on, we will teach you the rest of the tradition so you will know exactly what to do. We won't leave you clueless. Now,.for the rest of the gifts."

Pryce speaks up and says:

"YOU MEAN THERE'S MORE?! OH NO! PLEASE DON'T DO ANYTHING ELSE! YOU'LL HAVE DONE ENOUGH ALREADY!"

"No, we haven't. We have something else for you. If you looked inside the cars, you noticed on the seat an envelope. Inside is a year supply of gas and maintenance on your vehicles. Also, your incurance is paid up for three years. And last but not least, here is another envelope for you. They open it and it reads:

MORTGAGE PAID FOR THREE YEARS. ENJOY YOUR NEW LIFE TOGETHER WITH ONE LESS THING TO WORRY ABOUT!

Troy replies for everyone by saying:

"You guys are too much! This is unbelievable. We thank God for all of you and pray that God continues to Bless You from the top of your heads to the soles of your feet. We love you more than you will ever know and that will never change. Thank you so mech!"

"You are so welcome. But we need no thanks." responds Rick.

They enjoy the rest of their evening. About midnight, the newlyweds finally leave the hotel and return home to get ready for work the following morning.

The staff is happy to see Jada coming back to work on Monday morning. They hug and smile and make all kind of noise until the boss comes in and says they have to get back to work or get another job.

They just look at him, get real quiet for a minute, and keep doing what they are doing. So, he just joins in on the fun. He has no authority at all, he should have known that.

It is a long day for Jada. On the drive home she gets a call from Troy, asking he out to dinner. She tells him she's tired and just wants to go home and relax. He says he will pick something up and she shouldn't worry about cooking

"Jada"

today. She is so relieved she doesn't have to cook today that she almost shouts.

Jada gets home before Troy and has time to take a shower and relax a minute before he comes in.

"Hey Baby."

"Hey Troy. How was your day Sweetheart?"

"It was good. I don't need to ask you how your day was."

"Oh, Baby, I am so beat. You will not believe my day."

"Well, you sit there and relax and I will fix you something to eat. How about that?"

"Troy, I am really too tired to eat right now. Can I eat later? You go on and eat."

"No Babe, I'm going to wait on you. I'll get you a glass of wine."

"Thanks Baby. I wish it had some alcohol in it."

They both laugh and sit down with their "NON-ALCOHOLIC" wine. Jada lays on Troy's shoulder and they start to watch the news on TV. It didn't take but 20 minutes and they were both asleep. When they awoke, it was 10 PM. They decide to get some appitizers, more wine, then go to bed.

Troy goes in to take a shower, and when he returns to the bedroom, Jada is fast asleep. He sets the alarm so they can get up for work the next morning to start their day all over again.

God's Promises

In the morning, Jada is going to get up and fix coffee. On the way to work, Troy is going to pick Donnavon up. They ride together now since they are going to the same place. Pryce goes to work in the opposite direction so she and Jada drive alone.

Two years have gone by since they got married. One morning Jada gets a phone call from Pryce asking her to take her to see her doctor. She is so sick. Jada calls off work so she can take Pryce to her appointment.

Pryce is running a fever, has abdominal pain, and vomiting. She has gotten so weak because she can't keep anything down. She has also gotten dehydrated. When she came out of the doctors office Jada ask her what the doctor said. She says:

"Jada…..you are not going to believe this. I have a virus and…….. I am 6 weeks pregnant."

"WHAT! ARE YOU SERIOUS?! PRYCE! THAT'S GREAT!"

"I know, and Donnavon is going to be so thrilled. He has been talking about a son for a year now. He will be so excited when I tell him. I can't wait to get home. I am so sick though, we won't be able to celebrate."

"Don't worry about that. When you get better we will turn the town out. I promise you that."

"Jada"

"Thanks Jada. Let's get out of here."

That evening, Troy gets off work early and goes home to help Jada fix dinner for Donnavon. They tell him it is Donnavon's birthday because they want to tell Donnavon first about the baby.

After getting dinner ready Troy goes to pick Donnavon up at work. When Donnavon walks into the house he sees Pryce sitting on the sofa.

"How are you feeling Honey?"

"I am better Babe. Are you hungry? Jada made dinner for us."

"That is sweet of her. I'll have to call and thank her later. Baby what did the doctor say? I tried to call you a couple of times but it went straight to voice mail."

"He said I have a virus."

"Oh, ok. We can handle that. You will start feeling better in a couple of days."

"I hope so Don. He told me too that I am 6 weeks pregnant."

Donnavon pauses with his mouth open and just looks at Pryce. He can't move. He is frozen in time.

"Baby…..Baby….you okay?" ask Pryce.

"PREGNANT? YOU'RE PREGNANT? REALLY? ARE YOU SURE?"

"Yes Baby. I'm sure. Are you upset?"

"Upset? No, just the opposite. I'm estatic! I have never been happier! I am finally going to have a son!"

"WOAH! BABY, IT COULD BE A GIRL!"

"What? How? I mean….you know what I mean. I don't care what it is as long as it's healthy and looks just like my beautiful wife."

"Oh, thank you so much Baby. That is so sweet."

He takes her in his arms and hugs her ever so gently and kisses her on her forehead.

"I love you Pryce, more than anything in this world."

"I love you too Donnavon."

CHAPTER XVI

Isaiah 9:6a
"For unto us a child is born, unto us a son is given:"

Great Joy!

      The weeks with Pryce's pregnancy seem to go by so fast. She is now 16 weeks and she is feeling this pregnancy as if she is ready to deliver. She is on her way to pick Jada up for a doctor's appointment because Jada's car is in the shop and won't be ready for a couple of days.

    Jada has been having headaches and abdominal pain for the past three days. Troy feels it's time for her to go get checked out. He thinks it might be her appendix acting up.

    Jada and Pryce wait in the doctor's office for 45 minutes before Jada is seen. She is in with the doctor for 15 minutes when she comes back out. She has to go get blood work then come back to see the doctor. When she returns she has to wait another 30 minutes before being seen by the doctor.

Dr. John comes into the room and looks at Jada and says; "Jada, do you have an OBGYN?"

"Yes. I go to Dr. Jones. Why do you ask?"

"I am sending you to see him because your blood work doesn't look right. I want to make sure you don't have an infection. I will call and see if he can see you now. Wait here until I come back."

Dr. John leaves the room to call and make Jada's appointment with Dr. Jones. He returns to the room five minutes later and tells Jada Dr. John will be waiting for her.

Jada and Pryce head to Dr. Jones's office which is about 15 minutes away. On the way to his office Pryce tries to calm Jada down. She was so upset about the news she has just received.

They finally arrive at his office. They sit in the car for a while waiting for Jada to calm down before they go in. When she goes in the nurse asks her to sign in and have a seat. She waits 10 minutes before going in to see the doctor. This time she takes Pryce in with her. Dr. Jones entered the room with his nurse and ask her to get undressed so he can examine her.

"Jada"

"What are you looking for? What's wrong with me?" ask Jada.

"Don't get excited Jada. I just need to check and see what this infection is coming from. Your hemoglobin and iron are a little low, so I want to be cautious and make sure it is nothing serious. Will you lie back for me please?" ask Dr. Jones.

Jada lays back on the table and calls for Pryce to come and hold her hand. She is afraid she might have cancer and the doctors aren't telling her. She is shaking so badly that the doctor has to calm her down and get her blood pressure down before he can finish the exam.

"Okay Jada, you can sit up now. Okay you have nothing to worry about. Your uterus is enlarged and it will continue to enlarge until we remove the growth. It is a slow growing one so don't panic. It isn't something that has to be taken care of immediately. We will remove it in about……oh let's say…….seven months."

"Why are you going to wait so long? I don't want to wait that long. Can't we do it immediately?"

"I'm afraid not. We have to wait until it matures."

"What? Until it matures?! Have you lost your mind?!"

Great Joy!

Dr. Jones starts to laugh and reaches and grabs Jada's hand. "My dear Jada....there's nothing to worry about. You're pregnanrt."

"P...P.....Pregnant?! You're kidding? Aren't you?"

"No Jada, twelve weeks,"....says Dr. Jones.

"Jada! That is wonderful," says Pryce.

Jada doesn't know what to do or say. She is shocked, happy, surprised, and extacit all rolled up in one.

On the way to the car Jada is like a zombie. She is aimelessly walking along and Pryce has to guide her every step of the way. Pryce can't believe what she is seeing. She thinks Jada should be happy about the news. She doesn't understand what is going on with Jada so she decids to ask her.

"Jada, what is going on with you? I thought you would be happy with the news. Is something wrong? Did you not want to have children? Jada, I don't understand. What is it?!"

"Pryce.....I am happy. I just didn't think I could ever have kids. I never got pregnant so I didn't think I could become pregnant. Troy!!! I have to call Troy!"

"Jada! Please! Calm down! Here...here's your phone, call Troy. I will stay with you until Troy gets home so you won't be alone. You'll fall to pieces if you're alone. I don't know why, but you will."

"Thanks a lot Pryce. I don't know why I'm so crazy about this. I'm happy about it. What's my problem? Do you think Troy will be happy?"

"Of course he will. Now....call him and have him meet you at home because you have something to tell him that is very important. That way, he won't stop by my house with Donnavon."

"Good idea. I'll call him now."

Jada makes the call to Troy and tells him she needs to talk to him after work so he should come straight home. Troy is so nervous, he decides to get off work early. He thinks something might be wrong with Jada because he knows she isn't feeling well. She hasn't been feeling well for a few weeks. He knows she has a doctor's appointment too, so he is really nervous.

When Jada gets home, she is surprised to see that Troy is already home. Since Troy is at home, Pryce drops her off and heads home. She is really nervous about what Troy will say, but she has to tell him. This is suppose to be a happy moment for couples so why is Jada feeling like this about being pregnant?

CHAPTER XVII

Psalms 51:4
"Against thee, thee only, have I sinned, and done [this]
evlil in thy sight: that thou mightiest be justified when thou
speakest, [and] be clear when thou judgest."

Second Chances

*J*ada is so nervous and Troy doesn't know why. He is thinking the worst. Jada sits himdown and starts telling him about her situation.

"Troy, I need to tell you something. Don't say anything until I'm finished, okay?"

"Okay, I promise. Baby, what is it?"

"Troy, when I was 21 years old, I got pregnant. It was at a time in my life when I couldn't take care of myself....least of all a baby. I was having trouble with my fiancée` at the time and didn't know what to do. I didn't know God and wasn't in the so I was just lost. My only way out, I thought, was an abortion. I have never forgiven myself for that and I didn't think I would ever have children, because during that ordeal, I got a bad infection after the abortion."

"I never thought about having kids anymore because I thought God was punishing me. The doctor said I couldn't have children because the infection had done so much damage. So children never became a dream of mine, until now."

"I don't know how you feel about children Troy, and I should have told you this before we got married but it never dawned on me that this situation would come up until now."

"Troy, God is a God of second chances. The doctor told me today that I have a bad kidney infection and also that.... I am 12 weeks pregnant. Are you angry or upset with me Baby? I know I should have told you all of this."

"Jada, you're right. You should have told me about all of this. It might have been a stumbling block in our relationship. But Baby, I love you and it would not have mattered one way or the other. If you couldn't have children, it wouldn't have changed the way I feel about you. We could always adopt."

"Jada.....I love you.....nothing could or would have ever changed that. And in answer to your other question......I am very happy that we are going to have a little girl like you, or it can be a boy if you want."

They both laugh at what Troy's comment and he hugs and just looks at her and smiles while holding her. She feels all of he nervouseness leave because she knows at that point that God has given her a second chance and she is so thankful. She was especially thankful for her husband that God has sent her, who loves her. Unconditionally!

They sit on the sofa for a while untile Troy decides to go get dinner started. He is always pitching in to help with meals, especially since Jada has been sick.

"Do you want anything special Baby, or is it up to me tonight?"

"It's up to you this evening Troy. Whatever you conjour up is fine with me."

"Conjour? You act like I can't cook or something."

"No Baby, I am only kidding with you. I know you can burn in a kitchen."

"Alright Sweetie I know you are. Just lay there and I will get dinner started."

Troy prepares dinner and when it is done he takes Jada's to her in the living room, she is fast asleep. So he puts her food in the oven for her to give her a little more sleeping time.

After about an hour, he wakes her up to see if she is ready to eat, but Troy has already eaten his dinner. While Jada is

"Jada"

eating, Troy goes upstairs to shower and get ready for bed. When Jada finishes eating and cleaning up her dishes, she goes upstairs to join him.

When she gets upstairs she is so surprised. Troy has candles lit, soft music playing, and rose petals leading to the bathroom. The bathroom also has candlelight. There are bubbles in the tub and the scented candles have it smelling so nice in there. On the table beside the tub, there is a small glass table that has champagne on ice, chocolate covered strawberries, and one purple rose in a vase. She looks around and tears come to her eyes.

"Troy, what have you done? This is so lovely?"

"Baby you know how your family does things. I talked to Jason and he told me what you will like, and this isn't all. Get undressed and get into the tub."

Jada does what she is told gets into the tub. There are rose petals everywhere, even in the bathtub that was full of bubbles. Once she gets into the tub, Troy tells her to lay back and relax. Then he prodeeds to give her a foot and leg rub.

He begins massaging her leg with the warm water and bubbles from her thiaghs to the tip of her toes. He even massages her feet and each toe one by one. When he finishes that leg, he goes to the other leg. After that routine is done, he takes her to the bedroom and gives her a full body massage. Jada is so relaxed that she almost falls asleep on him.

After he is done with the massage, they drink the champagne accompanied by the strawberries and lay on the bed in each others arms and listen to the music and talk. Jada is so relaxed and stress free. They are both so comfortable that they fall asleep and don't wake up until the alarm goes off the following morning.

The months go by so fast and Jada's and Pryce's co-workers throw tham a baby shower. They only have a couple of weeks before they are due, and believe it or not, Jada is a whole lot bigger than Pryce.

Troy and Donnavon pick the girls up after work because they don't want them driving right now. Jada and Pryce worked in different locations until Pryce asked to be transferred downtown with Jada. The company had no problem doing that because she is such a good worker and dependable employee.

Troy and Donnavon gather up all of the girls belongings and put it in the cars. Pryce gets in the car with Jada and Troy because her car is so full of baby gear, including two strollers and two baby swings.

"Jada"

Time is winding down for Pryce to deliver and Jada isn't too far behind her so they decide to go do their last minute shopping. They wanted to get more bottles, diapers, a bath tub, t-shirts, blankets, and socks. They have some things but they want to make sure they have enough. They know if they have to send Troy aand Donnavon out to get something, God know what they will come back with. They do their shopping and head home so they can start dinner for the guys, who have gone to play golf like they do every Saturday.

On the way home Jada stopps at the grocery store to get some sugar and flour. When she pulls out on the highway her car stops in the middle of the road and she is T-boned by an Tractor Trailer Truck.

Jada and Pryce have to be helivacked to a nearby hospital. Both girls went into labor on the Helicopter and delivered before they could get to the hosoital.

Jada and Pryce are both unconscious and in serious condition. Jada doesn't know it but she has twins…..a boy and a girl. Pryce has a boy but he dies right after delivery. This is going to be very tramatic to Pryce when she wakes up.

Once the Helivac lands, the Flight Nurse gives the babies to the NICU Nurse to put in an incubator. The babies have not been name banded yet. The Flight Nurse tells the NICU

Nurse that Jada has a boy as she hands her the Mason babies. The NICU Nurse assumed one baby is Jada's Baby and put the wrong name on the babies.

The hospital calls Dr. Jones to let him know that Jada and Pryce have arrived and what condition they are in. Troy and Donnavon are also called and are on their way to the hospital as well.

When Troy and Donnavon arrive at the hospital they ask where their wives are. They are told they are in surgery, and Dr. Jones will be out to talk to them in a little while. They go get a cup of coffee and take a seat to wait on Dr. Jones to arrive. After about 45 minutes Dr. Jones appears from behind the double doors.

"Troy, Donnavon, .sorry to meet you like this."

"Dr. Jones, how are our wives, asked Troy?"

"They are going to be fine. They delivered a little early, but the babies are fine. Troy, you have a son and Donnavon, you have a daughter. They are both doing well."

"Can we see our wives now?"

"Not yet. They have just gone to recovery and as soon as they get them settled in, you can go see them."

"Okay, thanks. Can we see the babies, asked Donnavon?"

"Sure. Right this way. There is your daughter Donnavon. And Troy, your son is right over there. Oh…they must have him in the back bathing him. I will go check."

Dr. Jones comes back and tells Troy they can't find the baby anywhere on the floor. After checking the hospital and calling the police, they put out an Amber Alert.

"YOU LOST MY SON!!!!"

CHAPTER XVIII

Exodus 2:10
*"And the child grew, and she brought him unto
Pharaoh's daughter,
and he became her son."*

Missing

The hospital is filled with police officers looking all over the place for this little person that just came into the world in a very tramatic way. Jada hasn't been told yet that her son is missing and neither has Pryce. They don't want to traumatize them any more than they have to right now. Troy knows tht Jada will go into shock and literally have a heart attack.

The police ask Troy all kinds of questions. He is a lawyer so they want to know if he has any enemies that would want to get revenge or hurt him or Jada in any way. They talk to family members, friends, and co-workers. They haven't looked at the hospital cameras yet because they have to go to another building to get them. They send a detective to pick them up so they can view anyone who could have taken their son.

As Troy and the staff look at the video, one of the nurses notices a doctor she doesn't know. The rest of the staff looks and don't know her either. They call the Chief Of Staff to come and look at the video and he doesn't know her either. As they enlarge the picture, it becomes clear to Troy that he knows this women.

"WAIT! I KNOW HER! SHE WAS A CLIENT OF MINE IN A MALPRACTICE SUIT! We won the case but she became a fatal attraction and I couldn't get rid of her. She still sends me text messageses, calls and doesn't say anything and I know it's her. She leaves notes on my car, roses at my door and I am tired of her. Her name is Traci Cummings. She is employed by High Plains Medical Center in Atlanta, Georgia. Do you really think she took my son? She isn't stable."

"We don't know, but we have to look at all angles. Agent James, get out there and find this woman. If anyone can find her, Agent James can. Don't let the trail get cold." said the FBI Agent.

"Don't worry Mr. Mason, we'll get your son back. In the meantime, I think you need to tell your wives before someone else does."said Agent James

"Yes, you're right. We should go talk to the girls. Come on Donnavon, let's go tell the ladies what's going on."

They go to tell Pryce first and she doesn't take the news well at all. So they know what Jada is going to do. The doctor is with them in case he has to sedate them, and of course, he has to sedate Pryce to get her calmed down. After they get her calmed down and she falls asleep, they go break the news to Jada.

Troy sits down on the bed beside her and begins telling her the story. Jada tries to get out of bed so she can go searching for her baby. The doctor has to sedate her too and she falls asleep after a while.

Jada and Troy name their son Justin Troy, and Pryce and Donnavon name their daughter Zoe Danielle. It has been three days and the ladies are being discharged. There is still no news on Justin, but they are still looking and they think they are getting close to finding him.

It's been a week and Troy gets a phone call from Traci.

"Troy, Sweetheart it's me, Traci."

"Traci! What are you doing? Where is my son?"

"You mean our son Troy."

"Okay, where is he? Is he okay?"

"Of course he's okay. Why wouldn't he be? I want you to meet me after you get off work so we can have dinner and go to a movie like you promised me."

"Okay Traci. Where do you want me to me you?"

"Why at home of course. Where else?"

"Why don't you meet me at the restaurant? I have to work a little late. That way, we won't be late for the movie."

"Okay. Can we go to Bradigans."

"Sure, I will meet you there at five o'clock."

"Okay dear."

Troy hangs up the phone and his phone rings immediately. It was Agent James. He has traced the call and has some Agents on the way to Traci's house now. Troy calls Donnavon and tells him the news. Donnavon and Pryce head over to Troy's house to be with them until they hear something else.

After about an hour there is a phone call. It is Agent James. He tells Troy he has his son and is at the hospital with him and he should meet him there. They all get in the car and head to the hospital. Jada can't wait to get her hands on her son.

When they arrive at the hospital the doctor is checking the baby out to make sure he is okay. Once finished, the nurse brings little Justin out and gives him to Jada. She has tears running down her face. She is so happy. She holds him so close. Troy can't get close enough to the little body to hug him. So he settles for hugging them both.

They take their little bundle home and Traci goes to a mental ward. They don't have to worry about her any more.

As time goes by, things have gotten back to normal. Justin and Zoe are 2 years old now and attend daycare. The two of them are so attatched to each other. Everybody thinks they look so much alike not to be brother and sister. And, they are so close to be so young.

Pryce gets a call from daycare that Zoe has a fever and she needs to be picked up. Pryce picks her up and takes her to see her doctor. He gives her some antibiotics and does some blood work, then tells Pryce if her temperature doesn't go down, take her to the emergency room.

It is about midnight when Pryce checks Zoe's temperature. It is 104 degrees. She wakes Donnavon up so they can take her to the ER. She is admitted and more test are going to be run.

For some reason, Zoe has lost blood and needs a transfusion. Pryce and Donnavon go to donate blood but they find out they aren't a match. They don't understand why neither of them is a match for their baby girl. They call and tell Jada and Troy about the problem so they come to the hospital to get tested to see if they are a match. They are.

Troy is 100 percent a match. How can this be? Troy isn't the father, Donnavon is, and Pryce is the mother. What is going on? Zoe also needs to have a bone marrow transfusion. They do a DNA test to see what the problem is. They think the test is wrong.

The DNA testing comes back and it says Donnavon is not the father and Pryce is not the mother. It says 99.9 percent that Troy and Jada are the parents. Now they are really confused. Dr. Jones is called in on this case. He is told what is going on. Dr. Jones comes to the hospital to check out the records to see if he can straighten things out. He ends up calling the parametics who were on duty the night of the accident to see if they remember anything. There was only one on duty that remembered the whole thing, and she straightened up everything for him.

After a couple of hours, Dr. Jones calls the four of them back to the hospital to tell them what he found out.

"After the car wreck, the babies were delivered on the helicopter. Jada, you had twins. A boy and a girl. Pryce, unfortunately, your baby didn't survive. When the Flight Nurse gave the babies to the NICU Nurse, she didn't tell her they were twins and the name tags hadn't been put on them yet. She gave the nurse the mother's names as she handed the babies to her, and that's how they labeled the name tags on the babies. So Jada, both of these babies are yours."

"WHAT! I HAVE TWINS?! WE HAVE GONE TWO YEARS AND YOU LET PRYCE THINK SHE HAS A LITTLE GIRL!?

HOW CAN YOU MAKE A MISTAKE LIKE THIS!? HOW CAN YOU DO THIS TO HER!?"

"Calm down Jada, said Troy. We are going to get through this, all of us."

Pryce is in tears. She has lost the little girl that she has grown to love as hers. Donnavon is in shock too. They don't know what to say. They don't know how they are going to give her up. This is going to be the hardest thing they are ever going to have to do.

Troy and Donnavon go home and Jada and Pryce stay with Zoe. Jada tells Pryce she can see Zoe anytime she wants. And she can always be a part of her life.

Three years pass and Pryce and Donnavon have a little baby boy and name him Lance. They all stay close friends, just like family, and the children are close too. Through it all, God works it all out and love conquers all.

CHAPTER IXX

Luke 8:17
"For nothing is secret, that shall not be made manifest, neither anything hid that shall not be known and come abroad."

THE LAST PIECE OF THE PUZZLE

*J*ada is so happy with Troy and the baby, and by the way, she is pregnant again and due in about a month. She has everything she ever wanted. She does though have one thing that is weighing heavily on her. She wants DJ to tell her where her twin brother is so she can meet him. So, she is planning to go to his house and have a talk with him to see what they can work out.

Jaden was separated from Jada when DJ divorced their mother. They were too young to know about each other so they didn't search for each other. Jaden still doesn't know

The Last Piece Of The Puzzle

about Jada, but Jada does know a little about Jaden and wants desperately to find him.

That evening when she arrives at DJ's house they have a nice conversation about Jaden. She finds out that Jaden has been in the Air Force. After leaving the Air Force he joined the Police Department in Los Angeles. He has been on the Force for 9 years. He is married to a beautiful woman and her name is Zoe. They have two children: Clinton 18 and Desiree 16. Jaden is also a Minister, and has been for 12 years.

After Jada gets all of this information on Jaden she asks for a phone number. She wants DJ to call him and pave the way so she won't be such a shock to him. DJ agrees to call Jaden and gets the phone to call him at that moment.

"Hello." says a voice on the other end of the phone.

"Hello, Jaden?"

"Yes, this is Jaden."

"Hi Jaden. This is your Dad."

"Hi Dad. It's been a bit. How are you doing? It's good to hear from you. What can I do for you?"

"Jaden, I need to talk to you about something very important."

"Sure Dad. What's wrong?"

"Nothing is wrong. I need to tell you something."

"Jada"

"Okay Dad, you are scaring me."

"OH NO! DON'T BE SCARED. I need to tell you about the divorce between me and your mother."

"What? What about it?"

"Jaden, when your mother and I divorced, she allowed me to take you with me because you are a boy. She thought I could do a better job than she could because she is a woman."

"I know that Dad."

"Let me finish Jaden. You also have a sister that your mother kept because she thought she could do a better job because she is a woman. I tried to get her to let me take her too, but she refused. Your sister's name is Jada. She is an Attorney and a lovely lady. She's married, has one child, and one on the way in a couple of months. Jaden, she wants to meet you. I have told her all about you."

"WOW! A SISTER! ARE YOU FOR REAL? WHY AM I JUST FINDING OUT ABOUT HER?! DID YOU KNOW ABOUT HER ALL OF THIS TIME!?"

"Yes and no. But, can we talk about this in person?"

"Yes. I guess so. WOW! A SISTER!"

"Jaden, there is one more thing."

"YOU HAVE GOT TO BE KIDDING!"

"I don't know how to say this......but, Jaden...Jada is your twin sister."

"WHAT! OOOH! THIS KEEPS GETTING BETTER AND BETTER! WHAT ELSE ARE YOU KEEPING FROM ME DAD? AM I ADOPTED? ARE YOU REALLY MY FATHER!? THIS IS TOO MUCH! WHAT DO YOU WANT FROM ME?"

"Nothing son."

"DON'T CALL ME THAT!"

"I am sorry Jaden. I didn't think I would ever see Jada again. I looked for her everywhere. I never thought I would find her. I gave up and I shouldn't have. I am so sorry. I owe you both an apology."

"No Dad, you owe us more than that! You will never be able to give us back what we missed! Do you understand that?! Never!"

"I am truly sorry son. I have carried this around for years and it hasn't been easy to live with. I have always loved my children. I never wanted anything like this to happen. I wouldn't want to hurt either of you for all of the money in the world."

"Too late for that dad. We will talk soon."

"Jada"

DJ tells Jada that Jaden will meet with her. He also lets her know that Jaden is very upset with him and they both have a right to be.

Jada calls Jaden the following day and has a very nice talk with him. Jaden promises to come and visit with her and talk more later that evening.

Jada is getting some refreshments ready for Jaden and the door bell rings. How will this pan out for the two of them? Will they become close? Will time apart keep them apart? Are they twins but so very different? We shall see.

WHAT IS SARCOIDOSIS?

Sarcoidosis is a **Multi System Inflammatory Disease** that attacks the body's organs and systems. The white blood cells clump together and form into clusters called granulomas. These granulomas can cause permanent scarring. This Disease attacks the lungs in 95% of the cases. But it does attack other organs too. It is found mostly in African Americans and mainly Black females. This disease has been misdiagnosed as asthma, bronchitis, tuberculosis, and COPD and other diseases. There is not a lot known about this disease. They don't know what causes it and they don't have a cure as of yet. Prednisone is the drug of choice to help slow the progression of the disease.

Some **Signs** of Sarcoidosis are shortness of breath, fatigue, hacking cough, chest pain.

Statistics show:

- ❖ Prevalence of Sarcoidosis: 20 per 100,000 overall; 5 in 100,000 white people; 40 in 100,000 African Americans; 64 in 100,000 Scandinavians.
- ❖ Incidence extrapolation for USA for Sarcoidosis: 54,399 per year, 4,533 per month, 1,046 per week, 149 per day, and 6 per hour.

Death rate extrapolations for USA Sarcoidosis: 572 per year, 47 per month, 11 per week, and 1 per day.

To learn more about this deadly disease please contact:
Sarcoidosis Foundation of WV Inc at:
PO Box 7265 Charleston, West Virginia 25356

Or visit our website at:
www.wvsarcoidosis.org
e-mail at: snowflake@wvsarcoidosis.org **Or** yvonnelj3110@aol.com

CPSIA information can be obtained
at www.ICGtesting.com
Printed in the USA
LVOW13*2230040518
576048LV00002B/4/P